Argentine Radicalism:

The History and Doctrine of the Radical Civic Union

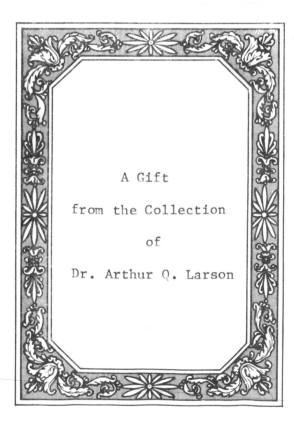

Radicalism is the historical current of the emancipation of the Argentine people, of the authentic realization of their life, of the cultivation of their moral welfare, and of the profession of their grand ideals. It has its roots in the history of nationality; it constitutes a requisitory against all material philosophies of human life and the destiny of the nation. Thus Radicalism is identified with the most noble sentiments of South American emancipation and the universal desire for the liberty of man.

Radicalism springs from the fountain of our history. Its affiliation is with the people in their long struggle to acquire personality. In the tradition that nourishes Argentine history, Radicalism is the organic and social current of the people, federalism and liberty. It interprets our emotional and human authenticity; it is the people themselves in their attempt to form a nation which is the master of its territory and its spirit.

Because of this the Radical Civic Union is not a simple political party, it is not a group that struggles for its own benefit, nor a composition that is dedicated to the acquisition of governmental positions. It is instead the patriotic mandate of our national solidarity, of the intransigence with which the radical sentiment of Argentine civic dignity can be fulfilled.

This is the reason why Radicalism is a concept of life, of the total life of the people. The Radical revolution, based on man and his liberty, is composed of all aspects of life from religion to economics. Radicalism is not partial to social classes, races or offices; it looks upon man as man, with dignity. For Radicalism the ends are inalterable: liberty and democracy for the integration of man. The means may vary because they are only instruments, and because the social conditions of the national reality will themselves vary.

The entire world is suffering from a profound illness which sprang from not using the modern material possibilities for the emancipation of man. Radicalism believes that only a great human crusade for the liberty of man against all the degrading forms of imperialism and absolutism, in all their aspects, will be able to save the world now in grave crisis. Radicalism renews its faith in the destiny of the people of our great continental brotherhood, united in their sovereign freedom, struggling to establish—with the instruments of political liberation—a system of social guarantees against all the economic privileges that deny liberty and negate justice.

(UCR Profession of Doctrinary Faith)

[iii]

ARGENTINE RADICALISM

THE HISTORY AND DOCTRINE OF THE RADICAL CIVIL UNION

Peter G. Snow

UNIVERSITY OF IOWA PRESS ᴪ IOWA CITY

To my parents

PREFACE

The study of Latin American political parties has been complicated to a certain extent by the great diversity of meanings that the word party can have when used in a Latin American context. A party may be merely an *ad hoc* group which puts a candidate in office—or attempts to do so—and soon thereafter disappears. At the other extreme, a party may be an evolving institution, such as the *Partido Revolucionario Institucional* of Mexico, with deep roots in the nation's history. Between these two extremes there are many different types of political organizations that are known as parties.

During much of the nineteenth century the political party alignment in Latin America was simpler than the multitude of party labels would indicate. In general an alliance of large landowners, high ranking army officers, and upper clergy—frequently called the Conservatives—was opposed by the business and professional groups of a more liberal attitude. Although this division has continued with certain modifications in Colombia, in most nations the Liberals and Conservatives were soon forced to share the spotlight with several new parties. Urbanization, industrialization, and the formation of a middle class and a class conscious proletariat combined to lead to a proliferation of parties in most Latin American nations. Some, such as the Socialists and Communists, were copies of European organizations, but others were almost completely indigenous; notable in the latter group are the Peruvian *Alianza Popular Revolucionario Americana* (APRA), *Acción Democrática* of Venezuela, and *Movimiento Nacionalista Revolucionaria* of Bolivia.

In Argentina an historical perspective will reveal parties of almost all the types mentioned above. Within this perspective, however, Radicalism occupies a special place. The *Unión Cívica Radical*, founded in the nineteenth century as a protest movement, has grown rapidly in power and prestige. Virtually all elections since 1914 demonstrate that Radicalism is a factor in national politics which must be evaluated in terms of its perennial strength. Although the party may not win all the elections, it has never been pushed into obscurity by any other party or combination of parties. In spite of these facts, very little has been written, in English, about Argentine Radicalism. It is hoped that this monograph will begin to fill this void by serving as an introduction to such a study.

CONTENTS

Chapter I

Parties and Politics: 1810-1890

In order to understand the motives behind the formation of the Radical Civic Union it is necessary to examine the political history of Argentina and especially the evolution of its political parties prior to 1890. Authorities differ greatly in their interpretaton of the origin of parties in Argentina. Some would go all the way back to the struggle for independence, while others claim that true parties were founded only after the overthrow of the dictator, Juan Manuel de Rosas, in 1852. The latter view would seem to be the more nearly correct, but earlier organizations still merit some attention.

Shortly after the war for independence had begun, two rival groups —or parties—were formed around the personalities of Cornelio Saavedra and Mariano Moreno. These were, respectively, the *Conservadores* and the *Demócratas*. The former, composed primarily of wealthy merchants and landowners and segments of the upper clergy, were interested only in independence from Spain—and some of them would not go even that far. They opposed any fundamental social, economic or political modifications. The Democrats, on the other hand, were desirous of real change. They wanted the war for independence to become a social revolution. An American writer has summed them up in the following manner: "Their creed was the Social Contract, their economic doctrine the free trade of the Physiocrats, their political philosophy that of the Encyclopedists, and their program essentially that of the French Revolution."[1]

These two groups are relatively unimportant as far as this study is

----

[1] J. Fred Rippy, *Argentina, Brazil and Chile Since Independence* (Washington, D.C.: George Washington University Press, 1935), p. 68. See also Segundo V. Linares Quintana, *Los partidos políticos* (Buenos Aires: Editorial Alfa, 1945), p. 85.

concerned, for after independence was attained the number one political question in Argentina was "what form of government shall the new nation have?" This question and the acute rivalry between Buenos Aires and the interior provinces absorbed all the energies of Argentine political groups until the rise of Rosas. In general, the partisans in this conflict are called Federalists and Unitarians, but this can be somewhat misleading for there were fundamental differences between the Federalists of Buenos Aires and those of the other provinces. It may be less confusing to look at this as a three-way conflict involving Buenos Aires Federalists, provincial Federalists, and Buenos Aires Unitarians.

The conflict was ideological as well as pragmatic. In general, the Federalists tended to equate federalism with democracy and liberty; they remembered the intense centralism of Spain and its dominions, and wanted no part of a continuance of a unitary system. The Federalists also recognized the economic and social differences between some of the provinces, especially between those of the interior and Buenos Aires, and felt that a federal system was best adapted to recognize these differences. On the other side of the fence, many of the Unitarians were convinced that only a unitary system could weld the warring provinces into one united nation. They were afraid that if federalism were adopted there would really be no nation.

On the pragmatic side, the conflict revolved primarily around the fact that the dominant source of income for Argentina was composed of import duties collected at Buenos Aires, which had the only developed port in the new nation. During and immediately after the revolution the river provinces were in extremely bad shape financially. They were cut off from their traditional markets in upper Peru, and their products going up and down the Paraguay and Paraná Rivers had to pay import and export taxes to Buenos Aires. The entire sum of the revenue collected at the Buenos Aires port was kept in the treasury of that province, a fact which certainly did not endear the *porteños* to the people of the other provinces. On the other hand, Buenos Aires had borrowed a great deal of money from England, and the only source of money for repayment was the port duties.

The *Unitarios* of Buenos Aires wanted to form a strong national government, but a government run by and for the people of Buenos Aires. Under such a system they could see to it that the revenue collected at Buenos Aires remained in their province. The *porteño Fed-*

erales actually favored a confederal, not a federal system. They tended to think of the people of the other provinces as uncivilized, and they wanted to have as little to do with them as possible. They were especially opposed to any form of union that would force them to share the port revenues with these "uncivilized ones." To the political leaders of many of the provinces federalism meant only provincial autonomy, the right of the *caudillo* to exploit his province. The spirit that later led to the Argentine nation, however, came from some of these provincial leaders.[2]

The federal-unitary conflict was laid aside when Rosas came to power, in spite of the fact that his tyrannical rule was ostensibly in the name of federalism. For seventeen years the brutal dictatorship of Rosas precluded the possibility of the development of real political parties. Only with the overthrow of the dictator in 1852 did party politics return, and then it was force and not ballots that decided issues for several years.

Beginning in 1852 there was a period of near anarchy in which the old struggle between Buenos Aires and the provinces was revived. In Buenos Aires a new Liberal Party, which was the heir to the old Unitarians, was led by Bartolomé Mitre. It was opposed by the provincial Federalists under the direction of José Urquiza.[3] For almost a decade both Liberals and Federalists were intent upon settling their differences on the battlefield instead of at the polls. Finally in 1861 Mitre's forces won the battle of Pavón, and Buenos Aires Liberals were firmly in control of the situation. Liberals even gained control of many of the provincial governments.[4] The final blow to the Federalists came in 1870 when Urquiza died, depriving them even of a rallying point.

For about nine months after the battle of Pavón Mitre was the *de facto* President of Argentina as well as *de jure* Governor of Buenos Aires. He called for the election of a new Congress which met in late May of 1862 and promptly chose Mitre to be the legal President of the nation. (His legal term ran from 1862 until 1868.) One of the first questions facing the new Congress was the site of the national capital. To the surprise of many, Mitre supported dissolution of the Buenos

---

[2] See Ysabel Fisk Rennie, *The Argentine Republic* (New York: The Macmillan Co., 1945), p. 36.

[3] The Federalists were themselves divided into Conservatives and Progressives, but this split was primarily a matter of the "ins" and the "outs" as far as provincial government was concerned.

[4] Linares Quintana, *op. cit.*, p. 91.

Aires provincial legislature and federalization of the city. The national Congress—which was then meeting in Paraná—readily supported this, but according to the 1853 constitution the plan had to be approved by the Buenos Aires legislature, and it refused to give its assent. This latter group instead issued a counter proposal: the national government was to be the guest of the provincial government in the port city for five years (1862-1867), after which period the question was to be decided by joint action of the legislature and Congress.[5] Congress agreed to this compromise but it was eighteen years, not five, before the issue was finally settled.

This conflict soon occasioned a split in the ranks of the Liberals. Those who wanted to dissolve the provincial government of Buenos Aires and make the city a federal district formed the *Partido Nacionalista* under the leadership of Mitre. Those who wanted Buenos Aires to remain the capital of the province formed the *Partido Autonomista*. This group was led by Adolfo Alsina. The members of these parties were often called *mitristas* and *alsinistas*. The Nationalist Party "was oriented toward national unity maintaining the hegemony of Buenos Aires—actually just the commercial elements of the city—over the rest of the nation, [while] the Autonomist Party defended the rights of the province of Buenos Aires over the city itself, and over the rest of the provinces."[6]

In 1873 another party, *Partido Nacional*,[7] was formed to back the presidential candidacy of Nicolás Avellaneda, who had gained a degree of prominence as Minister of Education under President Sarmiento. The party did not last long for Avellaneda soon made a deal with Alsina whereby those men merged their parties to form the *Partido Autonomista Nacional* (PAN). This new organization then nominated Avellaneda for the presidency and an Autonomist, Mariano Acosta, for the vice-presidency. In the presidential election of 1874 these PAN candidates easily defeated Mitre who was the Nationalist

---

[5] Several conditions were attached to this proposal: the provincial government was also to continue to reside in Buenos Aires; the city was to retain its representation in the provincial legislature; all provincial agencies in the city were to remain under provincial control; and the system of municipal government was to remain unchanged. See Austin F. MacDonald, *Government of the Argentine Republic* (New York: Thomas Y. Crowell Co., 1942), pp. 76-77.

[6] Rodolfo Puiggrós, *Historia crítica de los partidos políticos argentinos* (Buenos Aires: Argumentos, 1956), pp. 73-74. Written by a well-known communist official, this is probably the best single work on Argentine political parties.

[7] Not to be confused with Mitre's *Partido Nacionalista*.

nominee. Mitre and his Nationalist Party then turned to revolution; their revolt was put down in September, 1874, but for the next three years there was an almost continuous threat of a revival of violence. The imminence of civil war decreased considerably in 1877 when President Avellaneda managed to bring together Mitre and Alsina in the so-called "Concilliation of Parties."[8]

This Concilliation produced a split within PAN. Several of the former Autonomists, including Aristóbulo del Valle, Leandro Alem, Hipólito Irigoyen and Roque Sáenz Peña, left to form the Republican Party. These Republicans favored provincial and municipal autonomy and opposed all pacts or agreements between parties; however, their fundamental reason for being was a continuance of the fight against federalization of the city of Buenos Aires. They were convinced that the Concilliation with Mitre meant that the *alsinistas* had given up this fight.

The political situation in Argentina was complicated in 1878 with the death of Alsina, who was to have been the 1880 presidential nominee of the Concilliation. Mitre's Nationalists nominated the Governor of Buenos Aires, Carlos Tejedor, who was defeated by the PAN candidate Julio A. Roca. Mitre's followers again answered electoral defeat with revolution, and again their revolt was put down. The defeat of Tejedor at the polls and on the battlefield, and federal intervention in Buenos Aires province, signaled the demise of the Nationalist Party.

The PAN managed to gain the federalization of Buenos Aires in 1880, forcing the provinicial legislature to move to La Plata. With this old issue finally settled there was no reason for the continued existence of the Republican Party, which soon faded from the political scene. Thus with the disappearance of the Nationalists and Republicans the PAN was virtually unchallenged.

With the election of Roca in 1880 PAN became the "official" party; its dominance was accentuated after the election of Miguel Juárez Celman in 1886. It was the *único* (only) party and President Juárez was in complete control of it, thus the terming of his administration the *unicato*.[9]

Unicato is a quite accurate description of the Argentine government

---

[8] See Lázaro B. Grattarola, *Partidos políticos* (Santa Fe, Argentina: Imprenta de la Universidad Nacional del Litoral, 1952), p. 76.

[9] Puiggrós [*op. cit.*, p. 84.] says "political parties were born, lived and died in the period from 1860 to 1890."

[5]

under Juárez Celman. The governmental machinery of the entire nation revolved around the person of the president. In the provinces, the legislators were usually subservient to the governors to whom most of them owed their election. The governor was also very influential in the selection of national congressmen from his province. "His" legislature chose the senators, and he and the political party had virtual control of the election machinery so that "safe" men were elected to the Chamber of Deputies. The governors were in turn almost the personal agents of the president. It was not too difficult for him to keep them in line with the use—or just the threat—of his power to intervene in the provinces. The system was self-perpetuating; the president and governors managed to keep each other in office through the use of force, violence, and fraud.[10] As José Ingenieros said, "Argentine politics during the 19th century has been the monopoly of one social class—the landowners—at whose side lived crowds of mestizos that were neither a middle class nor a proletariat."[11]

At the same time that the government was becoming more autocratic and even less responsive to the people—if such was possible—the Argentine society was undergoing a change. A large part of this change was due to the formation of a middle class.

This new middle class was formed to a large extent from European immigrants. Immigration, which began in the 1850's with little more than a trickle, increased rapidly for the next forty years. In 1870 it amounted to 40,000 and in 1885, 109,000 immigrants arrived.[12] Most of these immigrants were from Italy and Spain; the rest, about 30 per cent, came mainly from France, Belgium, and England.[13] Most of them evidently settled in the city or province of Buenos Aires although many also went to Santa Fe.

They took up land, they opened small shops, they bought property, they saved their money. By the end of the century they were the most stable element in the community. . . . In commerce and industry foreigners outnumbered criollos three to one. . . . In medicine they outnumbered Argentine doctors five to one. They predominated in the construction industry, in

[10] José N. Matienzo, *El gobierno representativo federal en la República Argentina* (Madrid: Editorial América, 1917), p. 214.

[11] José Ingenieros, *Sociología Argentina* (Buenos Aires: Editorial Losada, 1946), p. 68.

[12] *Segundo Censo de la República Argentina* (Buenos Aires: [n.p.], 1898), II, clxxvii; III, cxlii, clxiv.

[13] *Anuario del Departmento Nacional de Estadística Correspondiente a 1893,* (Buenos Aires: [n.p.], 1894), p. 476.

transport, in whatever was not the care and feeding of cows and harvesting of crops. They even went into agriculture, not as holders of enormous latifundia, but as small tenant farmers raising grain and fruits. . . . The immigrants were the middle class. . . .[14]

This new immigrant group was not willing to accept the passive position of the Argentine lower classes. Its members wanted a voice in the government, yet the only important political party, the PAN, represented primarily the *estanciero* interests. There was thus no organized group for them to appeal to. In the last half of the 1880's, the financial situation in Argentina pointed up the apparently hopeless position of the middle class.

From 1881 to 1884 the paper peso had been convertible to the gold peso at par, but during the latter year, the government stopped conversion. Inflation then began. At this time, Argentina had a very unfavorable balance of trade and a great deal of gold had to be shipped abroad. Instead of calling in currency to keep it stable, the government issued more. The printing presses must have worked overtime. In 1885 it took 120 paper pesos to buy 100 in gold; the next year it took 144.[15] Imports continued to exceed exports; gold was shipped abroad at an ever accelerating pace. Now it should be noted that the ensuing inflation spiral did not affect all Argentines alike. The *estancieros* benefited greatly from it. They were selling meat and hides abroad for foreign currency and converting this into depreciated pesos. The greater the inflation the more pesos their francs and pounds would buy. The merchants were at the other end of the scale, however. The goods they imported had to be paid for in pesos and thus were becoming more and more costly—not only to them, but to their customers. Since the government seemed to be by, of, and for the *estancieros*, the middle class apparently had to sit back and await financial ruin. This it was not willing to do.[16]

On August 20, 1889, a banquet was held in Buenos Aires supposedly to celebrate the "adhesion of the nation's youth to the person of Miguel Juárez Celman, President of the Republic;"[17] the main purpose, how-

---

[14] Rennie, *op. cit.*, p. 166. See also, pp. 160-165.

[15] *Anuario del Departamento Nacional de Estadística Correspondiente a 1893*, p. 473.

[16] For an excellent summary of this financial crisis, see Rennie, *op. cit.*, pp. 176-181.

[17] Alberto M. Etkin, *Bosquejo de una historia y doctrina de la Unión Cívica* (Buenos Aires: El Ateneo, 1928), p. 45.

ever, of this meeting was to push Ramón J. Cárcano for the presidential nomination of the PAN.[18] This banquet is of little importance except for the fact that it set in motion a series of events that soon led to the formation of Argentina's most important political party.

On the same day that the Cárcano banquet was held, an article written by Francisco A. Barroetaveña, entitled "Tu Quoque Juventud," appeared in *La Nación*. This article was a condemnation of the meeting of the *juarista* youth. Its importance lies in the fact that it brought Barroetaveña to the attention of many other young men in Buenos Aires who shared his hatred of the *unicato* of Juárez Celman. This small group, supported by Senator Aristóbulo del Valle and Leandro N. Alem, planned a meeting similar to that of the *panista* youth, but in protest against the present government. The invitation issued by Barroetaveña on August thirtieth said:[19]

The independent youth of the capital are invited to a meeting that will take place in the *Jardín Florida*, next Sunday, September 1, 1889, at 1:30 PM in order to proclaim with firmness the resolution of the youth to exercise the political rights of citizenship, animated by grand ideas, with complete independence from the constituted authorities, and in order to awaken the national civic life.

This meeting at *Jardín Florida* was attended by at least two thousand persons, most of whom were university students or recent graduates. Speeches were given by Barroetaveña, Manuel A. Montes de Oca, Damian M. Torino, Del Valle, Alem, Pedro Goyena, Vicente F. López, Delfin Gallo, and Torcuato de Alvear.[20] General Bartolomé Mitre and Bernardo de Irigoyen were due to speak, but illness kept both of them away. Their speeches would probably have been very similar to those given, all of which criticized the administration in general and Juárez Celman in particular, and reminded their listeners that national renovation was up to the youth of the country.

Out of this September 1 meeting came the *Unión Cívica de la Juventud* (UCJ). Historians are fond of stating that this group had

---

[18] Cárcano soon removed himself from the race when on April 14, 1890, he wrote to President Juárez Celman stating that he would not under any circumstance accept the party's presidential nomination.

[19] As quoted in Carlos J. Rodríguez, *Irigoyen: su revolución política y social* (Buenos Aires: La Faculdad, 1943), p. 61.

[20] For the text of these speeches, see Jorge W. Landenberger and Francisco M. Conte, *Unión Cívica: su origen, organización y tendencias* (Buenos Aires: [n.p.], 1890), pp. 8-20.

only two planks in its platform: free suffrage and honest elections. That this is somewhat of an oversimplification can be seen in the eleven-point program issued by those attending this meeting.

We Resolve:

1. To establish a political center in the capital with the name Civic Union of Youth.
2. To sustain, within the legitimate framework of our institutions, public liberty wherever in the nation it is endangered.
3. To raise as our banner the free exercise of suffrage without intimidation and without fraud, and to condemn all official intervention in elections.
4. To protest against all that disturbs or impedes the exercise of the right to vote, and to prosecute all who are responsible for such by all legal means.
5. To proclaim the purity of administrative morality in all its aspects.
6. To begin propaganda in order to raise the public spirit, inspiring in the citizenry a zeal for the exercise of their rights and a compliance in their civil duties.
7. To guarantee the provinces the full enjoyment of their autonomy and to assure all the inhabitants of the republic the benefits of municipal government.
8. To aid in the initiation of those things which will bring about national defense through the action of citizens.
9. To take an active part in electoral movements, considering the exercise of suffrage as a duty of citizenship.
10. To invite the independent youth in the rest of the republic to form political centers in accord with the propositions announced here.
11. To contribute to a general political movement that embodies the high goals that the independent youth pursues.[21]

The demands for free suffrage, honest elections, provincial autonomy, and municipal home rule have characterized the programs of the Radicals ever since that time, but the statement about "the purity of administrative morality" now seems somewhat hypocritical in view of the graft prevalent during the period of Radical control of the *Casa Rosada*. Also, the promise to take active part in elections must soon have embarrassed the party since it abstained from almost all national elections until 1914.

The *Unión Cívica de la Juventud* spread amazingly fast. Within four months there were fourteen local clubs in the nation's capital, and the next year provincial clubs were opened in Salta, Esquina, Tucumán, Colón, Rosario, Córdoba, Mendoza, Villa Casilda, and San Luis;

---

[21] Quoted in W. R. Peralta, *Historia de la Unión Cívica Radical* (Buenos Aires: Imprenta G. Pesce, 1917), p. 27.

in Buenos Aires province alone there were fifty-nine clubs by the end of 1890.[22]

The first project of the UCJ was the registration of as many citizens as possible. In this connection, Barroetaveña, as President, issued a manifesto to the people asking them to get their names on the voting lists so that they could vote. This circular also told the people why they should not vote for the present administration. It began: "With the high and noble purpose of correcting these evils that afflict the Argentine populace, originated as a result of the abuses of officialism and popular indolence, the Civic Union of Youth issues this call to all good citizens inciting them to a great regenerative work. . . ."[23] This "regenerative work" consisted, of course, in "kicking the rascals out."

The next step was the formation of a real political party, which the UCJ was not. As early as December 20, 1889, Barroetaveña suggested that the youth join with the older, more experienced men who had addressed them at the September first meeting.[24] To effect this union, a meeting was held April 13, 1890, at the *Frontón Buenos Aires*. Here the *Unión Cívica* was formed. According to the Directive Commission of the UCJ, the purpose of this meeting was "to form the General Committee that will direct the political work of the *Unión Cívica de la Juventud*."[25] The newly formed *Unión Cívica* was to have three branches: a *Junta Consultativa* of five men including Mitre and Bernardo de Irigoyen; a *Junta Ejecutiva* of ten men headed by Leandro N. Alem; and a *Comisión de Propaganda* of 400-500 members headed by Luis Sáenz Peña. The old *Unión Cívica de la Juventud* continued to exist under the leadership of Barroetaveña for a short period, but as its membership overlapped that of the *Unión Cívica*, it soon dissolved.

Alem's first act as President of the Civic Union was the issuance of a manifesto on April 17, 1890, in which he condemned the government in power and set forth the goals of the new party:[26]

The government of the Republic is characterized by . . . ineptitude . . . and immorality in public administration . . . suppression of free suffrage,

---

[22] For the formation of the clubs in the capital, see Landenberger and Conte, *op. cit.*, pp. 49-72; for the provincial clubs, see *ibid.*, pp. 153-174.

[23] "Manifesto a los Electores de la Capital, 16 de noviembre de 1889," reprinted in Landenberger and Conte, *op. cit.*, pp. 73-75.

[24] Peralta, *op. cit.*, p. 49.

[25] "Manifesto de 8 de abril de 1890, Comisión Directiva de la Unión Cívica de la Juventud," reprinted in Landenberger and Conte, *op. cit.*, p. 77.

[26] Rodríguez, *op. cit.*, pp. 84-85.

and moral decadence. . . . The UC reclaims freedom of suffrage, effective responsibility of public administration, a more pure administrative morality, suffrage free of violence, and fraud, and respect for provincial authority.

A week later at a banquet given in his honor he explained the means that should be used to bring this about. "The *Unión Cívica* must bring about the social and political regeneration of the Republic by inculcating in the citizenry civic virtues and moral resistance to corruption."[27] This may have been the ideal method, but Alem and the other members evidently had little faith in such passive means, for they had already begun the preparations for a revolution.

In December, 1889, General Manuel Campos was approached by Alem and Demaría. He agreed to place his troops on the side of the revolutionaries and to lead the military campaign. Seven months were spent in planning the revolt. It was decided that there should be simultaneous uprisings in Buenos Aires, Rosario, and Córdoba. The revolutionists were convinced of success. After the military phase was over, Alem and Demaría were to become Provisional President and Vice-President, respectively, until honest elections could be held. The Revolutionary Manifesto was issued on July 26, 1890.[28] It shows the influence of Locke and Jefferson in its statements about the duty of citizens to depose tyrants and form a representative government. In most ways, however, it was quite typical of the Argentine or Latin American *pronuncimiento.*

The directors of the Civic Union, convinced of the absolute impossibility of obtaining by peaceful means political reparation that the honor and welfare of the nation demand, solemnly resolve a supreme and very sad sacrifice: revolution.

The revolution lasted only three days. The revolutionists lacked ammunition, and their plans were betrayed to the government.[29] On July twenty-ninth, the revolutionists put down their arms, and were guaranteed by the Juárez Celman government that no punitive action would be taken against them.[30] The next day a senator said, "The revolu-

---

[27] The full text of his speech is given in Landenberger and Conte, *op. cit.,* p. 151.

[28] It is reprinted in Landenberger and Conte, *op. cit.,* pp. 189-192.

[29] Most authors admit a lack of knowledge as to who betrayed the insurrection, but Manuel Gálvez in his biography of Hipólito Irigoyen claims that Irigoyen told a good friend of his about the revolutionary plans and this person in turn informed the government. (*Vida de Hipólito Irigoyen* [Buenos Aires: Talleres Gráficos G. Kraft], 1939, pp. 72-73.)

[30] This 1890 revolt has been the object of a great deal of literature. Some of the

tion is beaten, but the government is dead."[31] Juárez Celman resigned a week later. The *Unión Cívica* was pleased with this resignation, but according to Bernardo de Irigoyen, that had not been the purpose of the revolt: "The revolution of July did not limit its program to the removal of a man. . . . That movement was against a political system that prevailed in the capital and all the provinces."[32] The UC soon decided that the new President, Carlos Pelligrini, was not much of an improvement over Juárez Celman. The party then decided to carry its fight to the voters.

On January 15, 1891, an Electoral Convention of the Civic Union met in Rosario to nominate the presidential candidates of the party. All of the parochial clubs were represented. This was the closest thing to a national party convention that Argentina had yet witnessed. This convention named Bartolomé Mitre and Bernardo de Irigoyen as its standard bearers for the 1892 election. Mitre was in Europe at the time, but he returned on March eighteenth. Two days later he met with Julio Roca. They agreed not to fight at the polls for the presidency; Mitre was to be President and a *roquista*—not Bernardo de Irigoyen —Vice-President. On March twenty-first this *acuerdo* was announced.

This Mitre-Roca *acuerdo* split the new *Unión Cívica*. On June 26, 1891, the National Committee of the Civic Union met to discuss this accord. Of the fifty-six members, only the thirty-two who were opposed to the bargain attended. The twenty-four *acuerdistas* met separately, ratified the *acuerdo,* and established the framework of the *Unión Cívica Nacional.*[33] Two weeks later this UCN held a convention and replaced Bernardo de Irigoyen with Evaristo Uriburu as its vice-presidential nominee.

The rest of the members of the Civic Union who refused to accept

---

better works pertaining to it are: Juan Balestra, *El Noventa* (Buenos Aires: La Faculdad, 1935); José Nicolás Matienzo, *La Revolución de 1890* (Buenos Aires: [n.p.], 1926); José M. Mendia, *La Revolución,* 2 vols. (Buenos Aires: Imprento de Mendia y Martínez, 1890); Luis V. Sommi, *La Revolución del 90,* (Buenos Aires: Editorial Monteagudo, 1948); and Mariano de Vedia y Mitre, *La Revolución del 90* (Buenos Aires: [n.p.], 1929). Landenberger and Conte, *op. cit.,* reprints the manifestos (pp. 189-193, 197), a description by Del Valle (pp. 199-222), and all the decrees of the Revolutionary Government (pp. 193-194).

[31] Congreso Nacional, *Diario de Sesiones de la Cámara de Senadores,* 1890, III, 215.

[32] Quoted in José Bianco, *La doctrina radical* (Buenos Aires: Talleres Gráficos Argentinos de L. J. Rosso, 1927), p. 15.

[33] See Gabriel del Mazo, *El Radicalismo: ensayo sobre su historia y doctrina* (Buenos Aires: Editorial Raigal, 1952), p. 64.

the Mitre-Roca pact called themselves the *Unión Cívica Principista,* but they were called *Unión Cívica Radical* by the UCN and this is the term that stuck. This group, led by Alem, Hipólito Irigoyen, Marcelo T. Alvear, Bernardo de Irigoyen, and Lisandro de la Torre, held its convention on August fifteenth, at which time it nominated Bernardo de Irigoyen and Juan M. Garro as its presidential candidates. The UCR pledged its adherence to the principles espoused at the *Jardín Florida* meeting of 1889.[34] One author contrasts the UCN and UCR by saying that the *mitristas* wanted only peace and stability for the aid of the landed group and for foreign capitalists, while the UCR represented the youth of the nation and the small bourgeoisie who were looking for a democratic transformation of the nation.[35] It was certainly the UCR that carried on the ideals of the old *Unión Cívica de la Juventud* and *Unión Cívica.*

Mitre's pact with Roca and the PAN not only cost him much of his popularity, but also contributed to an outbreak of violence in some of the interior provinces. In some instances national troops had to be called in to put down anti-*acuerdo* uprisings. On October fifteenth, Mitre renounced his candidacy, and just five days later Roca resigned as President of the PAN. He gave as his reason the failure of the *acuerdo.*[36] This left Bernardo de Irigoyen as the only candidate.

On December eighteenth, the Governor of Buenos Aires announced the candidacy of Roque Sáenz Peña who was to be backed by a new party, the *Partido Modernista.* His candidacy was immediately supported by the governors of Santa Fe, Entre Ríos, Córdoba, Corrientes, and Santiago del Estero.[37] (These provinces plus Buenos Aires had 126 of the 232 electoral votes.) On February 15, 1892, Roque Sáenz Peña accepted the nomination of the Modernist Party.

President Pelligrini decided that the way to keep Roque Sáenz Peña from gaining the presidency was to nominate his father, Luis, as the PAN candidate. This would enable the "official" party to retain control of the *Casa Rosada.* Upon hearing of the pending nomination

---

34 See "Manifesto de la Unión Cívica Radical de 28 de agosto de 1891," reprinted in Bianco, *op. cit.,* pp. 30-31.

35 Puiggrós, *op. cit.,* pp. 90-91.

36 Letter to the Governor of Córdoba, Prospero Garcia, reprinted in Roberto Etchepareborda, "Acción opositora durante la presidencia de Carlos Pelligrini," *Boletín del Instituto de Historia Argentina,* III:7 (October, 1961), pp. 41-42.

37 During this period the support of a governor virtually assured a candidate of the electoral votes of that province.

of his father Roque withdrew his candidacy, and two weeks later, on March ninth, Luis Sáenz Peña was proclaimed the joint candidate of the PAN and UCN.

It is worth noting that Luis Sáenz Peña supported the *Unión Cívica* revolution of July, 1890, and had been mentioned as a possible vice-presidential nominee when the party convention was held in January, 1891. In fact after the Mitre-Roca pact was announced, Bernardo de Irigoyen proposed that Luis Sáenz Peña replace Mitre as the UCR presidential nominee. Luis wanted to be the candidate of all groups opposed to the *acuerdo,* but the UCR would not agree to such an alliance.[38]

The fraud and violence which prevailed during the provincial elections of March and Pelligrini's declaration of a state of siege shortly before the April election led to the withdrawal of De Irigoyen and to party abstention on election day. It had become obvious that the UCR could not expect anything approximating a fair count of the votes. This was the beginning of a long period of electoral abstention for the party.[39]

The UCR had the immigrant middle class as its primary basis of support. It was the urban merchants, clerks, and professional men, and the small landowners, especially in Santa Fe who were hurt the most by the financial crisis of the *noventa,* and it was this same group that lacked an organized political voice prior to the formation of the UCR. The leaders of the party were quite young—with the notable exceptions of Alem and Del Valle—and extremely idealistic. This youth and idealism were hallmarks of the party for many years to come.

It might be possible to trace many of the ideals of the party, and also several of its leaders, back to the Autonomists of Adolfo Alsina.[40] However, while it is true that Alem, Del Valle, Hipólito Irigoyen, and several others among the founders of the UCR had been members of the Autonomist Party, the arch enemy of the *Autonomistas* was Bartolomé Mitre whom the *Unión Cívica* chose as its first presidential candidate. Mitre was about as far removed from the ideals of the *Autonomistas* as any politician of that period. While the *Partido Autonomista* was not as liberal as the later UCR, the latter did incor-

---

[38] See Etchepareborda, *op. cit.,* pp. 32-33.

[39] The UCR did not enter a presidential election until 1916.

[40] Gabriel del Mazo sees *Autonomismo* as the precursor of Radicalism. See his *El Radicalismo: ensayo sobre su historia y doctrina,* p. 14.

porate some of the ideals of the intransigent wing of the former into its dogma. There were two fundamental ideas shared by these two groups: freedom of suffrage, and municipal and provincial autonomy. Also, both frequently let it be known that they were strongly opposed to alliances with other parties.

Chapter II

The Road to Power: 1890-1916

The father of the Radical Civic Union was Leandro N. Alem; he was "the leader, the program, and the symbol of the UCR, which was constructed and organized by him."[1] Alem was born in Buenos Aires on March 11, 1842; there is some question about his ancestry, but he was probably of Galician descent.[2] His father was a member of Rosas' *Mazorca (La Sociedad Popular Restaurador)*[3] and was executed for his activities in this organization after the fall of the dictator. Although Leandro was only eleven at the time of his father's execution, he did not soon forget the incident. Six years later he gladly volunteered to fight under Mitre against Urquiza's *Federales*.[4] He fought at the decisive battles of Pavón and Cepeda. After the victory of Mitre's forces was assured, Alem returned to Buenos Aires to complete his education. In 1869 he entered politics joining Alsina's *Partido Autonomista*. The only thing uniting the members of this party, other than the personality of Adolfo Alsina, was opposition to the federalization of the city of Buenos Aires.[5] For the first decade of his political career Alem's one goal was to keep Buenos Aires a provincial capital. In one of his many speeches on this subject he made this somewhat prophetic statement:[6]

---

[1] Alberto M. Etkin, *Bosquejo de una historia y doctrina de la Unión Cívica* (Buenos Aires: El Ateneo, 1928), p. 170.

[2] See Hugo Fernández de Burzaco y Barrios, *Los antepasados de Alem fueron Gallegos* (Buenos Aires: 1955).

[3] The *Mazorca* was a sort of 19th century storm troop. It was infamous for its violent attacks upon the critics of the Rosas administration.

[4] It was Urquiza that overthrew Rosas in 1852. See *supra* p. 3.

[5] There were few other issues separating Argentine political parties at this time.

[6] Quoted in Gabriel del Mazo, *El radicalismo: ensayo sobre su historia y doctrina* (Buenos Aires: Editorial Raigal, 1951), pp. 15-16.

If Buenos Aires is nationalized the central government will become the master of the port duties; it will become the center of almost all the wealth of the nation; the President will acquire an omnipotent power and federalism will be reduced to the letter of the constitution, to a submissive senate of the central authority.

After 1880 Alem reluctantly gave up his struggle against federalization of the port city, but he never relinquished the ideal that motivated this fight: the belief that local autonomy, through a federal system of government, was the best means of fulfilling personal liberty for the citizenry of Argentina.

Just three years after his graduation from law school Alem was elected to the Buenos Aires Chamber of Deputies and two years later he was chosen to represent that province in the national Congress. In 1877 when Alsina and Mitre announced their "Concilliation" Alem refused to accept the pact. He became one of the leaders in the organization of the short-lived *Partido Republicano*. This was the first of many occasions in which he refused to compromise his principles by agreeing to a pact between parties. It might be said that this was the origin of radical intransigence which was to become one of the hallmarks of the UCR.

Alem was elected to the national Senate in 1878, but he turned down the position in order to return to the Buenos Aires legislature and carry on his fight against the loss of the provincial capital. Two years later when federalization of Buenos Aires was an accomplished fact, he retired to private life, remaining almost completely divorced from politics until 1889, when he was instrumental in the founding of the Civic Union.

It is extremely difficult to decide just what formed the political principles of Alem. His writings and speeches are full of a mystique that renders some of them almost unintelligible. He was a disciple of the Kantian categorical imperative which he was desirous of transplanting to Argentine politics. He felt that politics could have no better base than these words of Kant: "Act only on that maxim whereby thou canst at the same time will that it should become a universal law." Alem wanted to bring morality into Argentine politics, and this idea permeates most UCR publications prior to 1946. Alem seems to have given the party a messianic fervor; to him the basic mission of the UCR was the reformation of Argentine morality. He refused to speak of the UCR as a political party, insisting that it was a movement whose goals were only partly political. This idea is found in the

[17]

speeches and writings of party leaders up to the Perón era.

The foremost UCR historian states that Alem established the two fundamental bases of the Radical[7] cause which are: (1) the concept of politics as an ethical movement and (2) the concept of federalism as an institutional form of Argentine sovereignty and personal freedom.[8]

In his preoccupation with the idea of ridding the nation of force and fraud, and establishing a government based upon morality, Alem had little to say about the functions of the type of government he envisioned. One sentence of his, however, probably sums up his views on this subject. "There should be as little government as possible because then man will have more freedom and will be able to rule himself, and his own initiative will be fortified and developed through his own activity."[9]

The most important figure in the UCR during the first forty years of its existence was the nephew of Leandro Alem, Hipólito Irigoyen.[10] He was born in Buenos Aires on July 12, 1852, to the sister of Alem and a French Basque who had been an active supporter of Rosas. After finishing high school Irigoyen managed to obtain a position as police commissioner in one of the small districts of Buenos Aires province. This position was probably obtained through the influence of Alem. In 1874 he entered law school, and although he later adopted the title of Doctor, it is doubtful whether he ever received his degree. He followed Alem into the Autonomist and Republican Parties and in 1878 was elected to the Buenos Aires legislature in a typically fraudulent election. Two years later he was elected to Congress where he served only one term before retiring from politics in 1882 to teach in a girls' normal school.

Irigoyen was one of the early members of the *Unión Cívica* and was as responsible as any single person for the split in the party in 1891. After the 1892 election he organized the UCR in Buenos Aires and soon became the principal political figure in that province. During his

---

[7] Radical is capitalized, even though this is not the real name of the party, in order to differentiate between members of the UCR and persons with a radical philosophy.

[8] Del Mazo, *op. cit.*, p. 11.

[9] Quoted in Alvaro Yunque [pseudonym for Aristides Gandolfi Herrero], *Leandro N. Alem, el hombre de la multitud* (Buenos Aires: Editorial Americana, 1953), p. 384.

[10] Hipólito spelled his last name Yrigoyen, but today it is more frequently seen spelled with the "I."

early political career the one ideal that dominated Irigoyen's thought was popular sovereignty. He was convinced that no government was legitimate unless it recognized the people as the ultimate source of authority. To him the solution for most of Argentina's political problems was quite simple—just institute a system of absolutely free suffrage. All of his efforts for many years were directed toward this goal. As far as he was concerned the method of selecting the government was more important than anything else.

* * *

On October 2, 1892, the National Committee of the UCR set November eleventh as the opening date for the party's National Convention.[11] There was at this time no real national organization, and the danger of fragmentation or even disintegration of the UCR was very real.

The 1892 National Convention framed a constitution for the organization of the party and established a set of principles which were supposed to explain the motives of its members. Organizationwise the UCR was to be composed of provincial conventions which chose candidates for provincial offices, Congress, and presidential electors; and a national convention which chose presidential candidates and wrote the national program. The day-to-day activities of the party were to be handled by a national committee composed of four delegates from each province chosen by the provincial conventions.[12] The 1892 convention did not adopt a party platform; it did issue a Declaration of Principles, but this gave little clue to the ideals of the UCR. This Declaration condemned the government, stated that the UCR would continue its struggle for liberty, and pledged its continued support to the principles of September 1, 1889 (which were nebulous enough in themselves).[13]

By 1893 the Luis Sáenz Peña administration was thoroughly discredited. The President had great difficulty in retaining a cabinet, and in July he turned to the UCR asking Aristóbulo del Valle to form a Radical ministry. Del Valle, who was competing with Irigoyen for leadership of the party, was unable to gain the support of the UCR.

---

[11] The leaders of the UCR never called it a party, but that term is used here for the sake of convenience.

[12] This constitution (*Carta Orgánica de la Unión Cívica Radical*) is reprinted in Del Mazo, *op. cit.*, pp. 312-315.

[13] This Declaration of Principles may be found in José Bianco, *La doctrina radical* (Buenos Aires: L. J. Rosso, 1927), pp. 49-50.

The party's National Committee voted unanimously against participation in the Sáenz Peña administration, and when Irigoyen was offered a cabinet post he replied, "Our mission is not to occupy government positions, but is the cardinal reformation of their organization as this is the only means of establishing public morality, republican institutions, and general welfare."[14]

On July thirtieth, the anniversary of the 1890 revolution, Radical-led revolts broke out in several of the provinces. In Buenos Aires the forces of Irigoyen took over La Plata, the provincial capital, and set up a Radical government. For several days Del Valle was able to convince the President not to intervene in the provinces nor send in federal troops to put down the revolts. However, Roca and Pelligrini soon persuaded Sáenz Peña to get rid of the Del Valle cabinet and send military interventors to Buenos Aires, Catamarca, Corrientes, San Luis and Santa Fe.[15] With the arrival of federal troops the rebel administrations were quickly removed and Conservatives returned to office.

Immediately after the failure of the 1893 revolts Alem started preparations for a new revolution. This time he was not able to enlist the aid of his nephew. Irigoyen did not specifically refuse to take part in another insurrection, but he did not attend the meetings of the revolutionary council nor did he do anything in Buenos Aires to prepare for armed conflict. It is probable that a successful revolution at this time would have placed Alem in the presidency, and some people feel that Irigoyen withheld his support for this very reason.[16] It appears that by this time Irigoyen had become convinced that he—and only he—could rescue the Argentine nation from its current state. His only rival for the leadership of the UCR was soon removed. After 1893 Alem became quite disillusioned, and on July 1, 1896, he committed suicide.[17]

The political maneuvering prior to the 1898 presidential election

---

[14] Quoted in Del Mazo, op. cit., p. 82.

[15] The Conservative leaders had threatened to start an investigation of past administrations and to begin with the actions of the President's son, who had been Minister of Foreign Affairs under Juárez. See Ysabel F. Rennie, The Argentine Republic (New York: The Macmillan Co., 1945), p. 193.

[16] See Rennie, op. cit., p. 192; and Manuel Gálvez, Vida de Hipólito Irigoyen (Buenos Aires: G. Kraft, 1939), p. 105. In spite of some defects this is probably the best of the many biographies of Irigoyen.

[17] In his obituary La Presna said "He is the apostle of the political and moral reaction of the Republic." (Quoted in Etkin, op. cit., p. 176.)

was quite similar to that which had taken place in 1891. In 1897 there were three political parties of importance in Argentina. By far the largest of these was the *Partido Autonomista Nacional* or PAN, led by Julio Roca and Carlos Pelligrini, both of whom were former presidents. Inside PAN there was a dissident sector which had retained the 1891 label *Modernista*; this group was composed primarily of the personal friends of Roque Sáenz Peña. The *Unión Cívica Nacional*, still led by Mitre, had great strength in the federal capital and in Buenos Aires, but was of little importance in the other provinces. The *Unión Cívica Radical*, although theoretically organized on a national scale in 1892, had very limited strength outside of Buenos Aires, and its electoral strength was further lessened by the division within the party between the followers of Bernardo de Irigoyen and Hipólito Irigoyen.[18]

Early in 1897 PAN held a national convention and nominated Roca as its presidential candidate. It was apparent that the only possibility of defeating him was through an alliance among all his opponents. For this purpose a meeting was held on August 15, 1897, between representatives of the UCN, the *bernardista* sector of the UCR, and the *Modernistas*. The leaders of these three groups were all present— Bartolomé Mitre, Bernardo de Irigoyen, and Roque Sáenz Peña. At this time it was decided that these groups should work together for the election of Bernardo de Irigoyen. In return for UCN votes for a UCR presidential candidate, the Radicals were to vote for Mitre men for positions in the Buenos Aires provincial government. It is not known exactly what the *Modernistas* were to receive from this alliance —other than the possible defeat of Roca whom they opposed.[19]

On September first, the UCR National Convention met in the capital to nominate a presidential candidate. After almost a week of debate, the convention voted sixty-five to twenty-two to meet with the *Modernistas* and UCN and choose a joint candidate to oppose Roca.[20] This attempt at united electoral action was doomed to frustration, because the Buenos Aires UCR refused to accept it. The *hipolitistas* of Buenos Aires did not attend the National Convention, and they controlled the UCR in that province. On September twenty-seventh the Buenos Aires Provincial Committee met and unanimously denounced any electoral

[18] These two sectors of the party have been called by various names, the most simple of which are *bernardistas* and *hipolitistas*.

[19] See Gálvez, *op. cit.*, p. 131.

[20] Etkin, *op. cit.*, p. 89.

pacts involving the UCR. This killed the proposed *acuerdo,* for if the UCR could not deliver the electoral votes of Buenos Aires, its candidate could not win.

The intransigence of the Buenos Aires Radicals was primarily the work of Hipólito Irigoyen. He had been bitterly opposed to an alliance in 1891 and he had not changed his mind in 1897. In the former year he preferred to relinquish an opportunity for the party to attain the presidency rather than yield on any of his principles. In 1897 he was willing to see the UCR torn in two and almost disappear; he would not relinquish his principle of intransigence.[21]

As a national political party the UCR was dead from 1897 until 1904; Irigoyen and his *antiacuerdista* followers in Buenos Aires killed it in the former year when they defied the will of the National Convention. Leandro Alem committed suicide in July of 1896, and Aristóbulo del Valle died in that same year. Bernardo de Irigoyen and his followers left the party after their 1897 pact with Mitre; Juan B. Justo left in 1894 to found the Argentine Socialist Party. And as a result of Irigoyen's intransigence in 1897, Lisandro de la Torre resigned from the party.[22] The resignation of De la Torre was perhaps the most damaging for he made it clear that he was leaving the party because of his conflict with Irigoyen. When Irigoyen and his Buenos Aires followers refused to attend the 1897 National Convention and instead sent a message refusing to accede to the pact with Mitre and Sáenz Peña, De la Torre sent his letter of resignation to the convention. It said in part:[23]

Dr. Hipólito Irigoyen has conquered us with his negative methods of resistance; he has defrauded the aspirations of the nation, without coming to the convention, without giving his reasons, without explaining his policy, without appearing in person to face an adversary capable of intelligent debate; the only reason he sent was his irreconcilable hatred.

---

[21] This principle was written into the *Carta Orgánica de la Unión Cívica Radical de la Provincia de Buenos Aires,* Article I, Section 26 of which says: "There shall be excluded all accords or transactions that might impede, at the present or in the future, the integral application of the principles that form the program of this party."

[22] Shortly before his death Alem said, "The conservative radicals will go with Bernardo [de Irigoyen]; other radicals will become socialists or anarchists. . . ." (Quoted in José Luis Romero, *Las ideas políticas en Argentina,* Mexico: Fondo de Cultura Económico, 1946, p. 216).

[23] Reprinted in B. González Arrili, *Vida de Lisandro de la Torre* (Buenos Aires: Talleres Orientación, 1940), p. 77.

The principles of the League of the South founded by De la Torre soon after this were not at all incompatable with the ideals of the UCR. It was just the conflict between Irigoyen and De la Torre that separated this party from the UCR. In fact when De la Torre later founded the *Partido Demócrata Progresista* he said that it "was founded to oppose the Radical Civic Union."[24] He might better have said that it was founded to oppose Hipólito Irigoyen.

In 1898 the UCR existed as an organized political force only in Buenos Aires; in fact for the next fourteen years there was no UCR organization in Salta, Jujuy, Catamarca, La Rioja, San Luis, Mendoza, Corrientes, San Juan, Tucumán, Santiago del Estero, and Entre Ríos.[25] Between 1898 and 1904 Irigoyen worked steadily at the rebuilding of the party, and at the same time he was preparing for another revolution. The UCR was reorganized around the Buenos Aires provincial section of the party which Irigoyen had led from the time of its formation in 1891. By 1904 Radicalism was once again a political force that had to be reckoned with, although it was still not spread as widely through the provinces as it had been a decade earlier. On February 26, 1904, the party's National Committee met for the first time in seven years; the main purpose of this meeting seems to have been to inform the people that the UCR was "back in business." Although Irigoyen was not a member of the National Committee, the manifesto issued by that body on February twenty-ninth espoused his ideas.[26] It asserted that the government was illegal and unrepresentative of the people, condemned all *pactos* and *acuerdos*, and demanded that all Radicals stay away from the polls in the national elections of that year.

At the same time Irigoyen was reorganizing the UCR he was also meeting with high ranking members of the armed forces in an attempt to gain their support for another revolution. On February 4, 1905, revolts broke out simultaneously in Buenos Aires, Bahía Blanca, Santa Fe, Mendoza and Córdoba. At first it appeared that the revolution might succeed. However, the success of the movement depended upon gaining control of Buenos Aires quickly, and this could not be done. Plans to seize the main government arsenal in that province were uncovered by the administration, and in a matter of a few hours the re-

---

[24] Lisandro de la Torre, *Los dos compañas presidenciales* (Buenos Aires: Colegio Libre de Estudios Superiores, 1939), p. 47.

[25] Matias G. Sánchez Sorondo, *Historia de seis años* (Buenos Aires: Agencia General de Librería, 1923), p. xxi.

[26] It is reprinted in Del Mazo, *op cit.*, pp. 323-327.

volt had failed there. When this news reached the interior the rebels soon gave up.[27]

By 1905 it was clear that Irigoyen had decided that he and the UCR should govern the nation or else refuse to have anything to do with the government. By this time the UCR probably would have had a large number of congressmen and several cabinet positions had the party been under the leadership of one of its more moderate members. Irigoyen, however, insisted on all or nothing. He seems to have worked more on revolutionary plans that would place him in the presidency than for electoral reform that would enable the UCR to come to power peacefully. This might explain the complete absence of a party program. The Radicals talked about popular sovereignty and administrative morality, but they did not attempt to explain to the people what political and economic policies they would follow should they come to power. In his manifesto of May 13, 1905, Irigoyen said that since the revolt had failed, the UCR would turn once again to the passive form of revolution—the boycotting of all elections.[28]

By 1909 not all members of the UCR were willing to go along with Irigoyen's policy of electoral abstention. In July of that year Pedro C. Molina resigned from the party because of its lack of a positive program. Shortly after this resignation, which was published in the party newspaper, *La República*, Irigoyen wrote a series of articles for the paper explaining that the UCR did not need an electoral platform because it was not a political party, but was "the nation itself."[29] Two months later another party leader, Leopoldo Melo, attacked the electoral abstention policy in a public manifesto. He pointed out that this was the policy of one man, Hipólito Irigoyen, and that the UCR was supposed to be the ultimate in nonpersonalist movements. This was the first time that the cry of *antipersonalismo* was raised in the UCR, but it was far from the last.[30]

In December, 1909, the UCR National Convention met for the first time since 1897. Little was done at this time, however, and the con-

---

[27] For a detailed account of this revolution see Ricardo Caballero. *Irigoyen: la conspiración civil y militar del 4 de febrero de 1905* (Buenos Aires: Editorial Raigal, 1951).

[28] Carlos J. Rodríguez, *Irigoyen: su revolución política y social* (Buenos Aires: La Facultad, 1943), p. 125. See also Luis Ernesto Rabuffetti, *El dogma radical* (Buenos Aires: Talleres Gráficos Argentinos de L. J. Rosso, 1943, p. 52.

[29] Quoted in Del Mazo, *op. cit.,* p. 128.

[30] Melo later became the UCR Antipersonalist presidential candidate who opposed Irigoyen in the 1928 election.

vention's only official pronouncement was a declaration which said nothing—except that UCR members would continue to refuse to go to the polls.[31]

* * *

The election of Roque Sáenz Peña on April 12, 1910, was a decisive event in the early history of Argentine Radicalism. The new President was well known by many of the leaders of the UCR. He had gone to school with Alem and served in the Buenos Aires legislature with Irigoyen; he had worked with several future Radicals in the Republican and Autonomist Parties.

Soon after his election Sáenz Peña met with Irigoyen. The President-elect offered the UCR positions in his cabinet, but Irigoyen replied, "Our determination not to participate in the government is immutable; the only thing that could change our resolution is honorable elections guaranteed by electoral reform."[32] The Radical leader had been offered cabinet positions in the past, and the fact that the new President was an acquaintance of his was not enough to make him desert his intransigence.

Roque Sáenz Peña was already convinced that the nation's electoral system needed revision; Irigoyen had only to convince him to make the changes desired by the UCR. The two men held a series of conferences on the subject of a new election law. While some persons claim that Irigoyen wrote the new statute, it is more likely that the two men agreed upon the general outlines of the law which was then drafted by one of the President's advisors. Irigoyen did insist upon one important point—there must be a guarantee of minority representation in Congress. Sáenz Peña wanted to retain the complete list system under which the party with the largest number of votes in each province obtained all the seats in the Chamber of Deputies from that province, but he soon gave in on this point. Eventually it was agreed that an incomplete list should be used in the selection of the lower house of Congress and presidential electors.[33] (Senators were to continue to be chosen by provincial legislatures.) It would seem that both men underestimated the future strength of the UCR. Sáenz Peña

---

[31] Caballero, *op. cit.*, p. 159.

[32] Del Mazo, *op. cit.*, p. 134.

[33] Section VI, Article 1 of the new election law said: "In the election of senatorial electors from the capital, national Deputies, and presidential and vice-presidential electors, each voter will be able to vote only for two-thirds of the number of persons to be elected . . . ."

would probably not have pressed for the complete list had he known that the Radicals would soon become the majority party in the nation's most populous provinces, and had Irigoyen forseen this event, he might well have welcomed the retention of the complete list.

The new election law—usually called the Sáenz Peña Law—was passed in three sections between July 4, 1911, and February 13, 1912. The law(s) provided for permanent registration (this was tied to registration for military conscription); a secret, obligatory, universal male vote; and the incomplete list.

It was generally assumed that the Sáenz Peña Law removed the barriers to UCR participation in elections, but this was not immediately the case. First of all, the new election law meant nothing if not fairly administered, and the UCR wanted some assurance on this point. Second, most of the members of the party wanted to be careful in the choice of which elections to enter first; they wanted their first showing at the polls to be an impressive one. And third, some of the UCR leaders were still opposed to the party's participation in elections.

The 1911 UCR National Convention spent most of its time discussing the possible effects of the Sáenz Peña Law—which had not yet been promulgated. The next major election was scheduled for March 31, 1912, in Santa Fe where the governor and vice-governor were to be chosen. When the President gave his personal assurance that the election would be absolutely honest, the National Convention agreed to enter candidates. It was not willing, however, to make a final decision pertaining to the congressional elections of April 7, 1912, so it delegated to the National Committee the authority to decide which, if any, provinces could enter Radical candidates in that election.[34]

Shortly thereafter, UCR provincial committees in Entre Ríos, Córdoba, San Luis, and La Rioja petitioned the National Committee for permission to enter candidates in the April election, but the committee refused to make any decision until it learned how the Santa Fe gubernatorial elections had been conducted. When the news of the UCR victory in Santa Fe reached the capital the committee met again.[35] Permission was granted to the provincial leaders in the federal capital

---

[34] See Caballero, op. cit., pp. 177-181.

[35] The approximate results of this election were:

Unión Cívica Radical	25,000
Coalición Conservador	20,000
Liga del Sur	17,500

and Santa Fe to enter a slate of candidates in the congressional elections, which were only four days off. At the same time it was announced that in the other provinces official party slates of candidates could not be nominated. The committee reminded all UCR members that since voting was now required by law they should go to the polls, but should vote only for Radicals. It was generally understood that in the provinces other than Santa Fe, UCR men would run for office, but not on an official party ticket. The election results could hardly have been more satisfactory for the Radicals who won the majority delegation from the capital and Santa Fe, and even elected one of their members in Córdoba, although he never assumed his seat in Congress.[36]

Until the results of the April seventh elections were made public the leadership of the UCR was split on the question of dropping the policy of electoral abstention. This split was apparent in both the National Convention of 1911 and the National Committee. The section of the party which wanted to continue to stay away from the polls was called the *rojos;* it was led by the original intransigent, Hipólito Irigoyen, who still opposed any participation in an administration not run by the UCR. The other sector, usually called *azules,* wanted to enter all elections after 1911 and to gain as many public offices as possible.[37] After the successes of 1912 Irigoyen and his followers were forced to give in on this issue, and the UCR ran a slate of candidates in almost all of the provinces in 1914.[38]

Roque Sáenz Peña died on August 9, 1914, and many feared that his electoral reform might be buried with him. However, the new President, Victorino de la Plaza, gave the nation his assurance that the elections of 1916 would be as honest as those under his predeces-

---

[36] Cámara de Diputados de la Nación, División Archivo, Publicaciones y Museo, *Composición de la Cámara de Diputados de la Nación por partidos políticos y distritos electorales 1912-1943* (Buenos Aires: Imprenta del Congreso de la Nación, 1956), p. 5. [Hereafter cited as *Composición de la Cámara de Diputados.*]

[37] Reds and blues were also the terms used to describe the old Federalists and Unitarians of the Rosas period. Some writers feel that there is a connection between the UCR *rojos* and the old *Rosistas,* but very little evidence of this is offered.

[38] In the congressional elections of that year the UCR won the majority delegations in Santa Fe and Entre Ríos and minority representation in Córdoba, Buenos Aires and Mendoza. This gave the party 29 seats in the 120 man Chamber of Deputies; the Conservative Parties with 25 seats were the only other group with representation in double figures. *(Composición de la Cámara de Diputados,* p. 7.)

sor. The UCR was willing to accept the promise of the new President, at least for the time being. On March 16, 1916, the party's National Convention met to choose its presidential nominee; there was little doubt in anyone's mind as to whom the convention would choose, but there was some doubt as to whether or not Irigoyen would accept the nomination. Of the 146 delegates 140 voted for Irigoyen, yet when a committee was sent to tell him this, he declined to accept, stating,[39]

In view of the honor that you have bestowed upon me by naming me your candidate for the Presidency of the Republic, I must comply with the duty of declining irrevocably this designation because of reasons which are absolutely identical to the motives that have determined my public activities. My thought has never been about governing the country, but about a plan of fundamental reparation. According to my judgment I must sacrifice the holding of any public office; thus I have always made it very clear that I would not accept a governmental position. My creed has been above all the vindication of the honor of the nation, and the restoration of its moral and public life. . . .

When this note was read to the convention another committee was sent to beg him to accept the nomination; he did so reluctantly.

The vote for a vice-presidential nominee was much closer (80 votes for Pelagio Luna and 59 for Vicente Gallo). This vote fairly well divided the *rojos* from the *azules;* the former voted for Luna and the latter for Gallo. The *azules* were opposed to Irigoyen as the presidential nominee, but they voted for him because they knew that they lacked the votes to select their own man, and they had high hopes that he would turn down the nomination. It is quite difficult to find ideological differences between the two sectors of the party at this time. The *azules* were opposed to Irigoyen, or at least to his almost absolute control of the party, but the opposition was not nearly as strong as it was ten years later. In general it was the *azules* who considered the UCR a political party and wanted to give it a definite program with which to attract more votes. A large number of the *rojos* thought of themselves as members of a movement that was eventually going to save the nation; they were not as interested as the *azules* in gaining office.

---

[39] Ismael Bucich Escobar, *Historia de los presidentes argentinos* (Buenos Aires: Ediciones Anaconda, 1934), pp. 464-465. It is entirely possible that Irigoyen preferred to come to power through a revolution rather than at the polls. The former would have been more likely to convince the people that the UCR was a regenerative force and not just another political party.

Although there were four candidates in the 1916 presidential election it was generally assumed that only force or fraud or a combination of the two could keep Irigoyen from the presidency. Neither was used —at least not to any great extent—and the UCR candidate received more popular votes than his three opponents combined; however, for a while it appeared that he had failed to obtain an absolute majority of the all-important electoral vote.[40] There were 19 UCR electors in the province of Santa Fe seemingly determined not to vote for Irigoyen, who needed all their votes in order to have an absolute majority. The Conservatives tried to obtain these votes, or at least to make sure that they did not go to Irigoyen. One of the electors was offered a signed blank check in return for his promise not to vote for the Radical leader.[41] The issue was in doubt until July twentieth when the electoral college met. The 19 UCR electors from Santa Fe all voted for Irigoyen thus giving him 152 of the 300 votes. As a result of the congressional elections of that year the Radicals increased their representation in the Chamber of Deputies from 28 to 47,[42] and although this was more than any other single party obtained, it was well under a majority.

❊   ❊   ❊

It is quite difficult to characterize the ideals of the UCR of 1916; its members insisted that it was not a political party and refused to publish a real program. The so-called program issued by the 1916 National Convention said:[43]

The National Convention of the Radical Civic Union, reunited by virtue of the dispositions of the organic charter, ratifies the fundamental propositions that have determined its convocation, and reaffirms categorically its will to comply with these propositions in the face of the resistance that threatens the integrity of its work of reformation. It declares its decision to realize a government based on the constitution which will be applied in its spirit, its text, its guarantees, and its rights, for the benefit of the individual and the nation and its provinces. This will be done in order to make the Republic a nation which is great in its institutions, strong in its

---

[40] According to Bucich Escobar, p. 466, the popular vote was:

Irigoyen (*Unión Cívica Radical*)	372,810
Rojas (*Partido Conservador*)	154,549
De la Torre (*Demócrata Progresista*)	140,443
Justo (*Partido Socialista*)	56,107

[41] Caballero, *op. cit.*, p. 241.

[42] *Composición de la Cámara de Diputados*, p. 10.

[43] Del Mazo, *op. cit.*, pp. 154-155.

culture and its riches, ennobled in the morality of its life and in the solidarity of the work of its dignified citizens.

And this was quite typical of the declarations of the members and organs of the party. In a search through a great many articles written by party leaders just prior to the 1916 elections the author was unable to find any clear exposition of the policies that the UCR planned to follow if elected. There were a very few statements which would throw some light on the subject, such as "moderate protection of industry is the economic policy best suited to young nations such as ours."[44] Much more common was the statement "the only program of the UCR is the restoration of the constitution and freedom of suffrage."[45] It is difficult to quarrel with success, however, and the UCR won the presidency in its first attempt, and obtained the largest congressional representation of any single party after entering only two elections.

In spite of the electoral success of the Radicals after the adoption of the Sáenz Peña Law, it seems quite possible that many of the votes cast for UCR candidates were primarily a reaction against the Conservative rule which appeared to many to benefit only the upper classes. The UCR had very little competition for the vote of the middle and lower classes. The Socialist Party was limited almost exclusively to the capital,[46] and the Progressive Democrat Party was a brand new organization appealing primarily to small farmers. In many areas there was virtually no choice for the voters who wanted to see the Conservatives removed from office—the UCR offered them their only hope.

---

[44] Ernesto Corvalán, "Pensamiento e ideas radicales, "*Revista Argentina de Ciencias Políticas*, X:58 (July, 1915), p. 412.

[45] José L. Cantillo, "Ideales políticas," *Revista Argentina de Ciencias Políticas*, X:58 (July, 1915), p. 339.

[46] It was 1924 before it elected its first congressman from one of the provinces (Córdoba), and 1932 before it received congressional representation from a second province.

Chapter III

The Radical Presidents: 1916-1930

When Irigoyen was inaugurated in October of 1916, he was confronted with Conservative control of almost all phases of the national and provincial governments. Conservatives had a large majority in the Senate while the Chamber of Deputies was composed of forty-three Radicals, nine Socialists, eight Progressive Democrats and fifty-five Conservatives.[1] The UCR was in control of the provincial governments of only Santa Fe, Córdoba and Entre Ríos. It must have been apparent to President Irigoyen that a Conservative Congress would block the passage of almost any reform legislation that he introduced, and as long as the Conservatives were in control of the provincial governments they were virtually assured of retaining control of Congress, especially the Senate (whose members are chosen by provincial legislatures). Thus, there was quite a pragmatic motive for intervention in the provinces.[2] However, it would appear that Irigoyen's intervention policy was based as much on principle as pragmatism. He felt that his election was a popular mandate, that the people wanted

---

[1] Cámara de Diputados de la Nación, División Archivo, Publicaciones y Museo, *Composición de la Cámara de Diputados de la Nación por partidos políticos y distritos electorales, 1912-1943.* (Buenos Aires: Imprenta del Congreso de la Nación, 1956), p. 10. Although opposed to the Conservatives, and in spite of the fact that their leaders were ex-members of the UCR, the Socialists and Progressive Democrats were bitter critics of the Irigoyen government.

[2] Intervention is the constitutional method by which the national government is able temporarily to assume control of the affairs of any or all of the provinces. When a state of intervention is declared, all provincial and municipal government in the province(s) is disbanded, and an appointive official with complete power is sent to the area. The intervenor is responsible only to the Congress or President (depending upon which one appointed him); he is under no compulsion to abide by provincial laws, and he remains in complete control until recalled by whoever appointed him.

him to begin the "national reparation" that he had long talked about. In this respect he said:[3]

I know well that I am not a governor of the common order, because there is no human power that could have persuaded me to take such a position. I am the enforcer of the supreme mandate of the people, whose duty it is to comply with the just and legitimate aspirations of the Argentine populace. Upon assuming this mandate I have contracted a new obligation which is the moral, political, and administrative reconstruction of the Republic.

As far as Irigoyen was concerned the governments of the eleven Conservative-dominated provinces were illegal and immoral because they did not truly reflect the will of the people. There was at least a degree of truth in this, for the Conservatives had long perpetuated themselves in office through the use of force and fraud at election time. However, the Radical leader had carried only three of these eleven provinces in 1916, and thus any popular mandate he received in the other eight must have been manifested in some manner known only to him.

Irigoyen's intervention policy is quite frequently criticized, and not just by his contemporary political opponents. It is often pointed out that he intervened in the provinces more often (twenty times) during his first term alone than had any two previous presidents.[4] His critics claim that the purpose behind this was the advancement of his own power or that of the UCR, and that he was destroying provincial autonomy instead of guaranteeing it. Not as frequently mentioned is the fact that between 1916 and 1922 the fifteen interventions by presidential decree all came while Congress was not in session and thus met the constitutional requirements.[5]

It is possible that the biggest mistake made by Irigoyen in respect

---

[3] Ismael Bucich Escobar, *Historia de los presidentes argentinos* (Buenos Aires: Ediciones Anaconda, 1934), p. 477.

[4] Between 1860 and 1916 there were sixty-seven interventions, or an average of one every ten months; between 1916 and 1922 the average frequency of provincial intervention was once every three and a half months. See Rosendo A. Gomez, "Intervention in Argentina, 1860-1930," *Inter-American Economic Affairs,* I:3 (December, 1947), p. 72.

[5] The 1853 constitution says only "The federal government intervenes in the territory of the provinces to guarantee the republican form of government, or to repel foreign invasions, and, on the request of their constituted authorities, to support or reestablish such authorities, if they have been overthrown by sedition or invasion by another province." (Part I, Article 6). The Argentine courts have ruled that if Congress is in session it has the exclusive power of intervention.

to provincial intervention was his timing. He waited for six months before intervening in Buenos Aires, and intervention decrees for the other provinces were dragged out for several months. Perhaps he should have removed the governments in all the provinces as soon as he took office, making it clear that he was doing so to turn over to the people the control of their local governments. Irigoyen does not seem to have been the type of person who coveted power for power's sake, and it is quite unlikely that his intervention policy was based solely upon partisan political goals—although this was a factor. It must be remembered that the President was an idealist, and that his announced goal upon assuming office was to make the government, national and provincial, responsible to the people.

In the congressional elections of 1918 the UCR gained sixteen seats in the Chamber of Deputies giving it a precarious majority in that house, and a combination of intervention and free elections enabled the Radicals to gain control of the governments of the national capital and the provinces of Mendoza, San Juan, La Rioja, Catamarca, and Buenos Aires.[6] In 1920 the UCR obtained 105 of 120 seats in the lower house; however, these figures somewhat exaggerate the party's strength for they include the Blue Radicals of Córdoba, the Official Radicals of Jujuy, Dissident Radicals of Santa Fe, White Radicals of Santiago del Estero, and Situationist Radicals of Mendoza.[7] In spite of his party's success at the polls, Irigoyen was never able to obtain a working majority in the Senate—thus negating the possibility of passage of his entire legislative program. The problem here was accentuated by the fact that his administration was opposed not only by the Conservatives, but also by the Socialists, who felt that his program did not go far enough in the field of social reform, and by the Progressive Democrats, who were simply anti-Irigoyen.

One of the primary areas of concern of President Irigoyen and the UCR was the improvement of the standard of living of the middle and lower classes. This might be considered a part of the President's overall program of returning the government to the people, or making it responsive to their desires. Almost as soon as he was inaugurated

---

[6] *Composición de la Cámara de Diputados,* p. 12; *Review of the River Plate,* XLIX:1372 (March 15, 1918).

[7] While there were few ideological issues separating these splinter groups from each other and from the main body of the party, their members were usually more loyal to local leaders than to President Irigoyen and thus could not always be counted upon to support the administration's program.

Irigoyen sent to Congress a series of bills which would have established a minimum wage, maximum hours, and workers' compensation insurance. Most of these early proposals were refused passage by the legislature, and of the few that became law most were declared unconstitutional by the Supreme Court, which still reflected the views of the Conservatives. Although the Radicals were unsuccessful in their attempts to pass minimum wage and maximum hours laws, some progress was made in this field during Irigoyen's first term without legislation. Average pay per day rose from three and a half pesos to seven and the average number of hours worked by urban laborers was reduced from ten to eight per day.[8] In 1921 a worker's code was finally pushed through Congress. Although not as comprehensive as Irigoyen would have liked, it did regulate working conditions, hours, and pay for minors, Indians, domestic servants and railroad employees; it also sought to guarantee a certain number of paid holidays and a degree of tenure.

In the field of education the first UCR administration was quite successful. A large number of schools were built, and the number of students attending public schools went up almost 50 per cent during the six-year period; at the same time the illiteracy rate was drastically reduced so that by 1922 less than 14 per cent of the Argentines were unable to read or write.[9] Even more notable perhaps was the university reform under which students were given representation on university councils and even some influence in the selection of professors. Also important was the fact that the opportunities for a university education were greatly extended.[10]

The record of the first Irigoyen administration in the field of public health was also quite good. A series of laws established maternity benefits and tuberculosis sanitoriums, an embargo was placed on the shipment of white phosphorus, a general sanitation bill was passed and an extensive water purification program begun. Not unrelated to

---

[8] Gabriel del Mazo, *El Radicalismo: notas sobre su historia y doctrina* (Buenos Aires: Ediciones Gure, 1957), p. 192. A significant part of these gains might be attributed to the generally increased prosperity following World War I.

[9] Alberto M. Etkin, *Bosquejo de una historia y doctrina de la Unión Cívica* (Buenos Aires: El Ateneo, 1928), p. 138.

[10] In order to fully appreciate the meaning of this reform one must be acquainted with the vast differences between United States and Argentine universities. The struggle for reform is presented in Gabriel del Mazo, *La reform universitaria* (Buenos Aires: Editorial Raigal, 1947).

these projects was the fact that the nation's mortality rate was reduced appreciably.

Irigoyen favored increased participation by the government in the nation's economy. While he did not propose nationalization of the nation's few industries, he did want the state to assume control of public services, some of the means of transportation, and the principal mineral resources. His policies in this respect were based not only on the belief that the state was best equipped to perform certain functions, but also upon a degree of economic nationalism. He was greatly opposed to the draining off of Argentine capital and resources to foreign countries. In general, his economic policies were opposed by the Conservatives, who claimed they were socialistic, and by the Socialists, who felt that they were far too conservative. His basic philosophy in this respect might be seen in some of his less cryptic speeches. In 1918 he said, "There is no duty more imperative than to take charge of the economic construction of the state."[11] And in a message to Congress two years later he said:[12]

The state ought to acquire a preponderent position in the industrial activities of the nation in order to respond to the public services, and in some areas these activities ought to be substituted for the application of private capital; in nations of constant and progressive development such as ours public services should be considered as principally the instrument of government.

Irigoyen liked to think of his administration as the arm of the people in their struggle against foreign exploitation. He was especially anxious to make sure that Argentine petroleum resources were not exploited by foreign companies. In September of 1919 he issued an executive decree stating that petroleum was the property of the Argentine nation and no longer open to private exploitation.[13] In 1922 *Yacimientos Petroliferos Fiscales* (YPF) was formed; this government corporation was given a monopoly on the production of all petroleum products. It soon became a symbol of defiance of foreign domination of natural resources. Ever since that date petroleum policy—and especially foreign oil concessions—has been a major issue in Argentine politics. For the last forty years it has been impossible for any Argen-

[11] Luis Ernesto Rabuffetti, *El dogma radical* (Buenos Aires: L. J. Rosso, 1943), p. 136.

[12] José Luis Romero, *Las ideas políticas en Argentina* (Mexico: Fondo de Cultura Económica, 1946), p. 221.

[13] See Gabriel del Mazo (ed.), *El pensamiento escrito de Irigoyen* (Buenos Aires, 1945), p. 90.

tine politician to talk about foreign oil concessions without the danger of losing a very large number of votes. This has become the number one symbol of economic nationalism.

The first UCR administration made some half-hearted attempts at agrarian reform, but very little was accomplished in this field. In his first message to Congress, Irigoyen suggested the reorganization of the Department of Agriculture and some reduction in the size of latifundia.[14] The goals of the agricultural policy of the President would seem to have been twofold: first, as might be expected, the return of the land to the people, and second, an increase in production. Almost nothing was done in respect to the former, for in addition to the bitter opposition of the Conservatives, the President came into conflict with the right wing of his own party on this issue. In an attempt to increase agricultural productivity the government assumed a monopoly on the export of cereals and set a minimum price for domestic sales. Production was increased during the first part of Irigoyen's term, but it was probably due more to the increased demand on the part of the Allied Powers than to governmental policies.

The first UCR administration, and the President himself, were frequently accused of being anticlerical, but this was primarily a political maneuver, an attempt to discredit the government. The UCR did contain several Masons, and the religious views of the Radicals were probably more liberal than those of the nation as a whole, but there was no anticlerical policy followed by the party at this time. The political opponents of the President pointed out that he did not attend church, but they did not mention the fact that he gave several important administrative posts to members of the clergy. Late in his first administration there was a great deal of talk in the Congress about legalizing divorce. President Irigoyen immediately sent a message to that body stating his opposition to such a measure. He said that the effects of legalized divorce would be detrimental to the homes and families of the nation. He also stated his opinion that such an act would work too fundamental a change to be accomplished by the legislative process, and that to be valid it would require a constitutional amendment.[15]

---

[14] Rodolfo Puiggrós, *Historia crítica de los partidos políticos argentinos* (Buenos Aires: Argumentos, 1956), pp. 143-144.

[15] Manuel Gálvez, *La vida de Hipólito Irigoyen* (Buenos Aires: G. Kraft, 1939), pp. 329-330.

In the realm of foreign affairs, the first problem facing Irigoyen was the position to take in relation to World War I. He inherited the neutrality policy of President De la Plaza, but while the neutrality of De la Plaza seemed to be based upon ignoring the war, Irigoyen proclaimed a "positive neutrality." Shortly after his inauguration he said,[16]

Our race, by its ethnic composition, is solidly European, but our nation is far removed from the spatial orbit within which the war is taking place. In their social makeup our people emanate from Europe, but in their political organization and in their new soul it is otherwise: a new culture has been born. We are moved by the war, but we will not be dragged into it.

A large majority of the Argentines were pro-Allies, but not even when German submarines sank Argentine merchant vessels would the President consider a declaration of war.[17] Whatever the motives behind his neutrality might have been, even his political opponents were forced to admit that it was a quite successful policy as far as the nation's economy was concerned. The Allied Powers bought virtually all the Argentine meat and hides that the nation could supply, and since Argentina was not then able to purchase Allied products in return, gold balances piled up in Argentine embassies abroad. The great profits from the war period were used to finance many of the domestic projects of the Radical administration. The war, however, did not bring prosperity to all Argentines. At the same time that wheat and meat were being sold abroad for huge profits, the greatly reduced imports brought about a scarcity of many items and serious inflation. The cost of living almost doubled.[18]

When the war was over Irigoyen objected strenuously to the linking of the League of Nations to the Versailles Treaty. In his opinion the victory of the Allies gave them no "rights" over the conquered nations. He felt that the peace treaty should be just a formal declaration that the war was over; he evidently would have preferred a return to conditions as they were before the war began. Irigoyen also had definite ideas as to the proper nature of a League of Nations. He wanted it to be composed of a General Assembly open to all nations on the

---

[16] Etkin, *op. cit.*, pp. 144-145.

[17] In several such cases he demanded and received reparations from Germany.

[18] Ministerio del Interior, Departamento Nacional del Trabajo, División de Estadística, *Investigaciones Sociales 1940* (Buenos Aires: [n.p.], 1941), p. 2.

[37]

basis of absolute equality, an Executive Council selected periodically by the General Assembly, and a Court of International Justice with the power of compulsory arbitration of all international disputes.[19] When he officially declared his nation's acceptance of the League of Nations Irigoyen made it clear that as far as he was concerned it was completely separate from the Treaty of Peace—he wanted no part of the latter. Even then he insisted upon quibbling over terminology; his pronouncement said, "Our nation adheres to, but does accede to, the pact."[20] On December 4, 1920, Argentina's chief delegate to the League of Nations, Honorio Pueyrredón, submitted a proposal to allow all nations to join the League. On the same day, and before the proposal could be voted upon, Pueyrredón officially announced the withdrawal of the Argentine delegation. On May 20, 1921, Irigoyen told Congress that he had recalled the delegates because the League would not accept ideas that he considered essential. He ignored the League of Nations for the rest of his term.[21]

In its relations with the other Latin American nations Argentina has traditionally attempted to assume the role of the big brother. Irigoyen was fond of speaking of the close ties that united the Hispanic nations and at the same time separated them from the United States. A good example of his feelings in this area is his attempt to hold a Congress of Latin American Neutral Nations in 1918. In May, 1917, Irigoyen asked the governments of the other Latin American nations (with the exception of Cuba which had declared war on Germany a month earlier) if they would be willing to meet in Buenos Aires to discuss Latin America's relationship to the war. Most of the nations approved of the idea in principle, and formal invitations were sent out for a meeting to be held in January, 1918. The Congress, however, never met. The United States let it be known that it was opposed to such a meeting, and several of the Latin American nations attached conditions to their attendance. Only Mexico sent a delegate, and this might be attributed to its desire to oppose the will of the United States.[22]

Perhaps the most often leveled charge against the first Irigoyen ad-

---

[19] Gálvez, op. cit., p. 295.

[20] Del Mazo, El Radicalismo, I, p. 247.

[21] Warren H. Kelchner, Latin American Relations with the League of Nations (Philadelphia: University of Pennsylvania Press, 1930), pp. 96-101.

[22] For an Argentine view of this ill-fated Congress see Del Mazo, El Radicalismo, pp. 294-299.

ministration was that of corruption. The President was not a part of it, and it is quite probable that he was blind to it even though it took place right in front of him. The members of the UCR, of course, denied all charges of corruption, and the other parties made wild charges with little basis in fact. An American author—not hostile in general toward the UCR—says:[23]

Argentina was treated to an orgy of spoils politics in which ministers lined their own pockets and found employment for their family and friends, and in which men who were mediocre or less than mediocre filled all the offices from school teacher to chemist. . . . The radicals had no organization beyond the discipline of Irigoyen's personal leadership, as was to be proven the day Irigoyen died. They had in their ranks a few men like Tomás Le Breton and Marcelo T. Alvear who were men of the Noventa and whom everyone respected. But the rank and file were political hangers on and with no interest beyond their personal gain. The intransigent men, the idealists, the men of the calibre of Justo and de la Torre, had been sacrificed to Irigoyen's dictatorial leadership, and were lost for good. And the day was coming when Alvear and the rest who were decent would go too. . . .

This is probably too critical of Irigoyen and too kind to the Radicals, who were soon to form the *Unión Cívica Radical Antipersonalista,* but it is indicative of the low quality of persons who composed the main part of the leadership of the UCR at this time. While the President was talking about the moral reparation of the nation many of his appointees were lining their pockets.

❊   ❊   ❊

Toward the end of his six-year term Irigoyen made some tentative overtures to the congressional leaders of the UCR to see if he could persuade them to amend the constitution in such a manner as to make him eligible for immediate reelection.[24] Somewhat surprisingly, nothing came of this plan, and when the UCR National Convention met in 1922 to nominate a presidential candidate, the delegates were forced to look beyond their long-time leader.

For all intents and purposes Irigoyen hand-picked his successor. When he let it be known to the delegates at the National Convention that he favored Marcelo T. Alvear, there was very little open opposition.[25] The delegates were not overjoyed at the nomination of Alvear,

---

[23] Ysabel F. Rennie, *The Argentine Republic* (New York: Macmillan, 1946), p. 214.

[24] Gálvez, *op. cit.,* p. 377.

[25] Alvear obtained 139 of the 185 votes cast for a presidential nominee.

whose political philosophy was virtually unknown to them, but to oppose him would have been to oppose Irigoyen. Marcelo Alvear was the aristocrat of the UCR. He had a famous name, immense wealth, and a great deal of land. He had spent much of his life in Europe as was customary for Argentines of his position. Alvear had been one of the original founders of the *Unión Cívica de la Juventud,* and had remained in the party ever since. One of the first Radicals elected to Congress after the passage of the Sáenz Peña Law, he served only one term before retiring. In 1916 President Irigoyen appointed him Ambassador to France and later as the nation's chief representative to the Versailles Convention.[26]

Alvear was opposed by four candidates in the general election, but the results were pretty much a foregone conclusion. UCR strength at the polls had increased steadily in the ten years that the Sáenz Peña Law had been in operation. The UCR nominee received over 55 per cent of the popular vote; the final results were:[27]

Marcelo T. Alvear	*(Unión Cívica Radical)*	458,457
Norberto Pinero	*(Concentración Nacional)*	200,080
Carlos Ibarguren	*(Demócrata Progresista)*	73,222
Nicolás Repetto	*(Partido Socialista)*	73,186
Miguel Laurencena	*(UCR Principista)*	18,435

In the congressional elections of the same year Radical representation in the lower house was increased from 84 to 91 (of 150 members).[28]

As far as party politics were concerned, the most important event of the Alvear administration was the split in the UCR—the formation of the *Unión Cívica Radical Antipersonalista.* There was dissention within the UCR from the time of its formation; splits had occurred in 1891 and again in 1897, but these were based primarily upon electoral policy and took place before the UCR had assumed a definite shape. In 1922 the UCR was the majority party in the national legislature, its leaders had occupied the *Casa Rosada* for six years and

---

[26] One of the best biographies of Marcelo Alvear is Felix Luna, *Alvear* (Buenos Aires: Libros Argentinos, 1958) although it is perhaps unnecessarily critical in places. Collections of his speeches and essays may be found in: *Acción Democrática* (Buenos Aires: Editorial Cultura, 1937); *Actuación Parlamentaria* (Buenos Aires: La Epoca, 1922); *Argentinos, Acción Cívica* (Buenos Aires: M. Gleizer, 1940); and *Democracia* (Buenos Aires: M. Gleizer, 1936).

[27] Bucich Escobar, *op. cit.,* pp. 495-496. (Alvear also received 235 of the 333 electoral votes.)

[28] *Composición de la Cámara de Diputados,* p. 18. Radical splinter groups held ten more seats.

were to remain for six more, and it was in control of the governments of most of the provinces. Thus the 1922-1924 split in the party assumed much greater importance than those of 1891 and 1897.

It will be remembered that at the UCR National Conventions of 1909 and 1912 a group of Radicals called the *azules* went on record as opposed to a continuance of the *hipolitista* policy of electoral abstention. In 1916 this same group tried to obtain the vice-presidential nomination for one of its own number, and acquiesced in the presidential nomination of Irigoyen only because it lacked the votes to block it. This *azul* group led by Gallo, Melo, Le Bretón and Cantillo, wanted the UCR to adopt a positive legislative program after the 1916 elections, but it was in a decided minority within the national party organization. Within the next few years, however, its members did manage to gain control of some of the provincial committees. In December of 1918 the *azules* of Buenos Aires issued a manifesto stating:[29]

(1)   Radicalism ought to be independent of all extraneous forces, especially personalism.
(2)   The separation of the party and the government ought to be absolute.
(3)   The party should immediately define its position in relation to the urgent political, economic, and social problems.
(4)   The radical ideal is to assure good public administration. It is the duty of the party to criticize those who do not fulfill these conditions.

Although President Irigoyen was not mentioned in the manifesto, it was obvious that a part of the UCR was not satisfied with his administration, and was not going to restrain future criticism of it.

Irigoyen's mistake in thinking that Alvear would be his puppet became apparent when the new President announced the composition of his first cabinet. Of eight ministers only one was a personal friend of Irigoyen; two (the military ministers) were not members of the UCR; and the other five were old *alemistas* who had opposed Irigoyen at various times. Alvear evidently realized that if he filled his cabinet with *hipolitistas* it would be Irigoyen and not he who governed. Irigoyen felt betrayed. He is reported to have said of one of the new ministers, "He cannot be a Radical, because he is an attorney for foreign companies."[30] With his chance to govern through the cabinet lost, Irigoyen's only real points of contact with the Alvear administration

---

[29] Del Mazo, *El Radicalismo*, II, p. 33.
[30] Gálvez, *op. cit.*, p. 380.

were the Vice-President and the Minister of Public Works who were old friends of his.

The split in the UCR became apparent to all late in 1922. There was a rather lengthy debate in the Senate over the seating of the newly chosen Alvearist senators from Jujuy. About the only charges against these men were that they were anti-Irigoyen. The debate pointed out which senators were still loyal to Irigoyen and which were ready to follow the new leadership of Alvear.

Early in 1923 a group of Radicals in the nation's capital formed the "Solid and Homogeneous Block," which declared its adhesion to Irigoyen and to his principles.[31] By this time virtually all of the UCR legislators were lined up behind Irigoyen or Alvear. Quite frequently the Conservative congressmen aligned themselves in support of the latter group. A formal split in the UCR became a foregone conclusion when the Conservatives and anti-Irigoyen Radicals joined forces in the summer of 1923 to change the rules of the Senate in order to deprive the Vice-President of his power to appoint committees. This was considered a direct insult to Irigoyen.

In 1923 and 1924 Irigoyen was still firmly in control of the national organization of the UCR, and thus it was the Alvearist group that was expelled from the party. The first meeting of the UCR Antipersonalist Party was held in Buenos Aires on August 23, 1924. There were representatives from the capital and all the provinces except Buenos Aires, Córdoba, Entre Ríos and Tucumán. At this meeting the party was formally organized under the leadership of Leopoldo Melo, Martín Torino, Segundo Gallo, and José Tamborini.[32]

It is somewhat difficult to determine the exact ideological positions that separated the UCR and the Antipersonalists, because a considerable number of the latter left the UCR solely because of their dislike of Irigoyen and his absolute control over the party. In general, however, the Antipersonalists were the more conservative and the less nationalistic of the two. Their conservatism is seen in the fact that on economic matters they were often in agreement with the Conservative Party. Most of the intellectuals, professors, and lawyers in the old UCR moved over to the Antipersonalists: this was also true of the old *alemistas* who had never been infatuated with Irigoyen.

As far as government policy was concerned one of the major points

---

31 *Ibid.*, p. 386.
32 Del Mazo, *El Radicalismo*, II, pp. 45-46.

of disagreement between the UCR and Antipersonalists was concerned with the exploitation of natural resources, especially petroleum. During Irigoyen's administration the UCR had made the state oil monopoly, YPF, the symbol of economic nationalism. The Alvear government desired the granting of private oil concessions, even if they had to be given to foreign companies. This difference in policy was also evident in other areas with the UCR favoring a much greater degree of state intervention in the nation's economy than the Antipersonalists. The foreign policies of the two parties were also different. The Alvearists had, for the most part, wanted to enter the war on the side of the Allies while the *hipolitistas* had insisted on a policy of strict neutrality. Alvear had opposed the withdrawal of the Argentine delegates from the League of Nations in 1920, and soon after his inauguration he saw to it that Argentina paid its past debts to the League. He also kept an unofficial observer at Geneva, but was unable to persuade the Congress to authorize the nation's active participation in the organization.[33]

The *hipolitistas* considered Alvear's administration "a reaction against the work of Irigoyen."[34] It is true that Alvear vetoed a law that would have required all wages to be paid in national currency, and that he was opposed to a national minimum wage law, but on the other hand his administration could not fairly be termed reactionary. Laws were passed which regulated the labor of women and children and night work in bakeries. A pension for bank employees was authorized. Also an inheritance tax was passed, and further progressive legislation enacted by many of the provincial legislatures.[35] In general, the Alvear administration was characterized by almost unprecedented prosperity. The value of land increased at an astronomical rate, and wages went up much faster than prices, thus giving the middle and lower classes perhaps the most comfortable standard of living they had yet enjoyed.

The results of the party split were shown in the congressional elections of 1924 and 1926. In the former year UCR representation in the

---

[33] Kelchner, *op. cit.*, p. 101.

[34] Lucia Tristan, *Yrigoyen y la intransigencia radical* (Buenos Aires: Indoamérica, 1955), p. 62.

[35] For a compilation of progressive legislation of this period see J. Fred Rippy, "Argentina," in A. Curtis Wilgus, ed., *Argentina, Brazil, and Chile Since Independence* (Washington, D.C.: The George Washington University Press, 1935), pp. 139-140.

lower house dropped from 91 to 72, and two years later it was reduced to 60. Very few of these seats were gained by the Antipersonalists, however. In 1924 they gained the minority representations from Corrientes and Entre Ríos and in 1926 they gained the majority seats from the latter province.[36] The Antipersonalists had much better representation in the Senate, due primarily to their control of several provincial governments by means of intervention.

As the elections of 1928 approached, the Antipersonalists had high hopes of retaining the presidency and increasing their representation in the Congress. The various conservative parties had formed the *Concentración de Partidos de la Derecha* and promised support to the Antipersonalist ticket of Leopoldo Melo and Vicente C. Gallo.[37] The combined vote of these parties in 1926 had exceeded that of the UCR by about 37,000 votes.[38] The Antipersonalists, however, overlooked the fact that Irigoyen still had a tremendous degree of personal popularity. When the votes were counted it was discovered that he and the UCR had carried every province but San Juan, and had received about 62 per cent of the popular vote and 245 of the 316 electoral votes.[39] The UCR also increased its representation in the Chamber of Deputies to 92, the largest number held by any single party up to that time.

The second Irigoyen administration was disastrous for the President's personal reputation, for the UCR, and for the nation as a whole. By 1928 Irigoyen was seventy-six years old and almost completely senile. He had never been able to delegate responsibility or authority, and during his second term in the *Casa Rosada* this meant that administration came virtually to a standstill. On top of this, Argentina entered the Great Depression at this time. Exports declined radically, and gold flowed out of the country so fast that the Conversion Office had to be closed. The corruption that had been so great in his first administration increased during his second. In one office of the state railroad there were three hundred employees where the law authorized

---

[36] *Composición de la Cámara de Diputados,* pp. 21, 24.

[37] Carlos R. Melo, *Los partidos políticos argentinos* (Córdoba: Universidad de Córdoba, 1942), p. 46.

[38] See Roberto Etchepareborda, "Aspectos políticos de la crisis de 1930," *Revista de Historia,* III (1958), p. 24.

[39] Bucich Escobar, *op. cit.,* pp. 528-529.   The official results were:

	Votes	Electors
Unión Cívica Radical	839,140	245
UCR Antipersonalista	439,178	71
Partido Socialista	64,422	—
Demócrata Progresista	14,173	—

six.[40] By 1930 revolution was in the air; virtually everyone expected it to come at any time—only President Irigoyen was oblivious to it.

The congressional elections of 1930 gave some indication of popular dissatisfaction, but not on the surface, for the UCR polled more votes than all the other parties combined. However, in 1928, the UCR had outpolled its combined opposition by 302,326 votes; in 1930 its majority dropped to 9,429.[41] The UCR lost the election in the nation's capital for the first time in fifteen years, and some of the UCR congressmen elected in 1930 were pledged to oppose Irigoyen. The party was coming apart at the seams; there were several factions in it, none of which were willing to follow the leadership of the aged President.[42]

On August 9, 1930, forty-four congressmen published a manifesto condemning the administration; on September third, the Minister of War resigned; two days later the Dean of the Buenos Aires Law School asked Irigoyen to resign for the good of the nation. He did so on that same afternoon, but it was too late to stop the revolution, and besides, the nation was no more interested in being governed by the Vice-President than by Irigoyen. On September sixth, a group of cadets from the Campo de Mayo Garrison, led by General José Felix Uriburu, marched into the capital and easily assumed control. The fourteen-year period of Radical administration was at an end.[43]

It is impossible to assign any single cause for the September revolution. There were several factors leading to the coup. The economic crisis was becoming worse almost daily and it was obvious that the President was completely unable to do anything to alleviate its effects. On top of the chronic depression the ever increasing corruption in the administration became intolerable. The alignment of ranking army officers with the landed aristocracy placed both force and wealth in opposition to the regime. The obvious senility of Irigoyen was also important, but it would seem that the most important single factor was that the nation as a whole had become disillusioned with the leadership of the UCR. The nation which had experienced only Conservative rule prior to 1916 expected miracles from the Radicals and they were not forthcoming.

---

[40] Rennie, *op. cit.*, p. 222.

[41] Etchepareborda, *op. cit.*, p. 32.

[42] Manuel Goldstraj, *Años y errores, un cuarto siglo de política argentina* (Buenos Aires: Sophos, 1957), p. 74.

[43] For a chronology of events leading up to this revolution see Roberto Etchepareborda, "Cronología Nacional," *Revista de Historia*, III (1958), pp. 144-155.

Chapter IV

Radicalism in the Second Conservative Era:
1930-1943

The revolutionary government of General Uriburu removed the Radicals not only from the presidential mansion and Congress, but also from all public offices. In addition to this, a great many members of the party were jailed or exiled. At the same time, Irigoyen was shuttled back and forth between jails for about two months and then interned on Martín García Island. He remained there—except for a few months in 1932 when he was allowed to return to his Buenos Aires home—until his death on July 3, 1933.

Irigoyen's dismissal from politics removed one of the major barriers to the reunification of the UCR. Almost as soon as the old intransigent was overthrown Alvear suggested that the UCR be reorganized in an attempt to reconcile the differences between *hipolitistas* and Antipersonalists. When the UCR National Committee agreed to this, both parties named delegates to a *Junta Nacional Pro Reorganización* which met during the first months of 1931. On May seventeenth of that year this committee issued a manifesto calling for UCR unity, reorganization of the party, and the espousal of a definite party program.[1]

By no means all of the Antipersonalists were willing to accept this reconciliation. Many who had left the UCR in 1924 because of their distaste for the leadership of Irigoyen were willing to return to the fold, but on the other hand, the more right-wing Antipersonalists who had worked closely with the Conservatives refused all invitations to

---

[1] See Gabriel del Mazo, *El Radicalismo: notas sobre su historia y doctrina* (Buenos Aires: Ediciones Gure, 1959), pp. 169-170. The last of these suggestions was an indication that the new leadership of the party was not to come from the *hipolitista* wing.

rejoin the UCR. The *Unión Cívica Radical Antipersonalista* continued to exist until the 1943 revolution, and even today there is a small group of Radicals who call themselves Antipersonalists and claim to be the remnants of the old party.

The UCR reorganization was not the only revamping of political party structure that took place subsequent to the 1930 revolution. The Socialist Party split in much the same manner as had the UCR a few years earlier, with the conservative sector of the party forming the *Partido Socialista Independiente.* At about this same time the various Conservative parties, most of which had operated only on a provincial level, joined forces as the *Partido Demócrata Nacional.* The Independent Socialists and National Democrats then joined the Antipersonalists in a loose alliance which they called the *Federación Nacional Demo-crático,* but which was commonly known as the *Concordancia.*[2] This alliance, like the old National Autonomist Party, was dominated by the large landowners. In order to combat the conservatives more effectively the Socialist and Progressive Democrat Parties joined forces under the label of the *Alianza Demócrata Socialista.* This alliance was never an effective national force, however, because its electoral support was limited primarily to the provinces of Buenos Aires and Santa Fe which were the strongholds of the Socialists and Progressive Democrats, respectively.

The first elections to take place after the 1930 revolution were held in Buenos Aires in April of 1931; and they were relatively free of fraud. This was not due to the government's desire to implement the Sáenz Peña Law but because fraud seemed unnecessary to assure Conservative victory. After all, the UCR was thoroughly discredited. The results were not at all what the provisional government had expected. The UCR obtained 54 gubernatorial electors, the Conservatives 49, and the Socialists 6. In spite of the long-standing antipathy between Radicals and Socialists the electors of the latter party were more likely to vote for a Radical governor than for the conservative candidate. Uriburu postponed the meeting of the electoral college and canceled elections in other provinces, which were to have been held that fall. This lesson was not lost on the Conservatives. Since it seemed entirely probable that their candidates could not defeat the Radicals in honest

---

[2] For a brief summary of the formation of this alliance see Carlos R. Melo, *Los partidos políticos argentinos* (Córdoba: Universidad de Córdoba, 1943), pp 47-49.

elections, the Conservatives went back to the force and fraud used prior to 1912.

The National Convention of the newly organized UCR met in September, 1931, to choose its candidates for the presidential election scheduled for November eighth. It nominated Marcelo Alvear and Adolfo Güemes. For the first time, the Radicals sanctioned an electoral platform. Prior to this the party had adopted only vague "statements of principles." The political program called for: limitation of the president's power of provincial intervention,[3] and of his power to declare a state of siege; direct election of the president, vice-president, and Senate;[4] full political rights for women; the transfer of the most populous territories to the status of provinces, and the representation of territories in Congress; and a greater degree of municipal autonomy.[5] Other sections of the platform advocated the nationalization of unused land; creation of national grain elevators; a minimum wage law based on the cost of living index in each locality; and collaboration with all international organizations.[6]

After the results of the Buenos Aires gubernatorial election, Uriburu was in no mood to take a chance on a UCR victory in the presidential race. On October sixth the provisional government announced that both Alvear and Güemes were ineligible for election—Alvear because six years had not elapsed since he left office, and Güemes because he was too closely associated with the second Irigoyen administration. When this announcement was made the UCR candidates resigned so that the party might choose someone that the provisional government would allow. However, the UCR National Committee declined to accept the resignations and instead decided to boycott all the 1931 elections.[7]

---

[3] Within ten days of his assumption of power, Uriburu intervened in all the provinces except San Luis which was already under Conservative control.

[4] Although the UCR obtained large majorities in the national elections held during Irigoyen's first term, it never obtained a majority in the Senate, whose members were chosen by the provincial legislatures.

[5] None of these were accomplished during the 1930-1943 period of Conservative rule.

[6] "Declaraciones de la Convención Nacional de 1931," in Raúl Guillermo Luzuriaga, *Centinela de Libertad: 1914-1940* (Buenos Aires: A. López, 1940), pp. 159-167. See also Eduardo Madariaga, "Caudillos y Programas," *Hechos e Ideas*, IV:14 (August, 1936), pp. 121-142.

[7] Not only was the President chosen at this time, but also the entire Congress and all provincial and municipal officials. Augustín Justo, the Concordance candidate, easily defeated Lisandro de la Torre, the nominee of the *Alianza Demó-*

Although the UCR leadership in 1931 was not *hipolitista,* the party was taken back to the policies and attitudes manifested by Irigoyen prior to 1916. During that period Irigoyen had employed abstention and nonalignment, but these were not instrumental in his election to the presidency. The UCR came to power primarily because of the fair and impartial administration of the Sáenz Peña Law, and the record from 1916 to 1928 showed that the party could gain office only when votes were honestly counted. It is true that after 1931 it became apparent that votes would not be counted as they were cast; however, the UCR could not hope to gain anything by a return to its pre-1916 policies. Radicals seem to have suffered from the delusion that they were returning to the policies which had been decisive in their first ascent to power.

Between 1931 and 1935 the UCR seems to have withdrawn from politics almost completely. The leaders of the party claimed that they were merely returning to the policies of Irigoyen, but the party no longer had a leader with the magnetic personality of Hipólito Irigoyen; nor could it claim to be the "regenerative force whose destiny it is to save the nation." The party had spent fourteen years in power and had accomplished relatively little. As far as criticism of the Justo administration was concerned, the Radicals certainly did not take full advantage of their opportunities. They did not even mount a concentrated attack on the Roca-Runciman Treaty.[8]

By 1934 the UCR was again in the midst of a troublesome intraparty dispute which was most pronounced in the nation's capital. The two factions of the party in that city were given the names *Legalistas* and *Mayoritarios* which were gradually adopted by Radicals in other sections of the country. Basically the Legalists were the old *hipolitistas* who had opposed the reorganization of the party in 1931, and wanted to continue the abstention policy indefinitely. This group seems to have been more interested in economic and social reform than in the right to vote or provincial autonomy; its members were

---

crata Socialista, in the presidential race, while the Concordance obtained 84 of the 158 Chamber seats to 57 for the Socialist-Progressive Democrat coalition.

[8] The main features of this treaty, signed in May of 1933, included: Argentina's agreement to give 85 per cent of the meat trade to foreign *frigoríficos* and reduction of its tariff on English goods to their 1930 levels; in return England agreed not to limit its imports of chilled beef to less than that purchased in 1932. The treaty was of value to the cattle owners but was of doubtful benefit to the nation as a whole.

still giving speeches of the same type that Irigoyen had delivered at the turn of the century. They looked at the September revolution and the Justo government as treason, as a sell-out to foreign imperialism. This was probably due, in a large part, to the petroleum policy of Uriburu and Justo, which was diametrically opposed to the nationalistic policy of Irigoyen.

The *Mayoritarios* were composed primarily of the Antipersonalists who rejoined the party in 1931 and hence were in favor of its reorganization in that year. These men, who had opposed the abstention policy from the beginning, were noticeably more conservative than the *Legalistas*. They talked a great deal about political democracy, especially free suffrage and strict adherence to the constitution, but they were not as interested in social and economic reform as were the Legalists. The 1930 revolution was considered by this group to be the consequence of *hipolitista* corruption. They were opposed to the Justo government, but were not able to criticise it as freely as they might have liked since the President was an Antipersonalist, who had served as Minister of War under Alvear—the *Mayoritario* leader.[9]

This intraparty conflict was quite evident at the 1935 National Convention, where the main issue was whether or not to continue the policy of electoral abstention. Most of the members of the National Committee, including Alvear, were in favor of going to the polls; however, such important leaders as Adolfo Güemes and Amadeo Sabattini were opposed to any change in policy, as was the left wing of the party in general. The *Legalistas* pointed out that the chances of honest elections were very slim. *Mayoritario* control of the convention was apparent when the delegates voted about two to one to go to the polls. Some of the *Legalistas* claimed that this was treason to the principles of Irigoyen; they felt that if the UCR entered elections and accepted the positions "given" to them by the regime, they would be giving their tacit approval to the electoral fraud and force employed by the government.[10] Instead, this group would have preferred to organize a revolution (which almost certainly would have met with the same fate as those of 1890, 1893, and 1905).

The UCR first entered the provincial elections in Catamarca, Entre

---

[9] For an excellent discussion of these two sectors of the UCR see Del Mazo, *El Radicalismo*, II, pp. 237, 273-275.

[10] See Manual Augusto A. Gondra, *Declinación del Radicalismo y política del futuro* (Buenos Aires: Ediciones El Mirador, 1957), pp. 14-15.

Ríos and Córdoba. In the first two provinces Radicals gained several seats in the legislature,[11] while in Córdoba, the UCR candidate Amadeo Sabattini, was elected governor. His platform was probably quite representative of the ideals of the *Legalistas*. It included the promise of a highly progressive income tax that could be paid for in land; the acquisition of land by the provincial government for distribution to small farmers; assurance of "permanent work" for farm laborers; and the promise of a continuing struggle against the public service monopolies.[12]

In the 1935 congressional election the UCR did better than its leaders had any reason to hope for. The party won about half of the contested seats in the Chamber of Deputies picking up the majority delegations in the capital, Córdoba, Entre Ríos and Santa Fe, and minority representation from Buenos Aires, Mendoza, San Luis, Santiago del Estero and Tucumán.[13]

In June, 1935, a group of young *hipolitistas* who were vehemently anti-Alvear, organized as a definite faction within the UCR. This organization called itself the *Fuerza de Orientación Radical de la Joven Argentina* or FORJA. Arturo Juaretche, the President of FORJA, characterized the program of the movement in the following manner:[14]

1. A return to the nationalistic doctrine of Irigoyen and the old federalist tradition of the pre-1853 era.
2. Acceptance of the ideological postulates of the 1918 University Reform.
3. A doctrine which is Argentine in its connection with Irigoyen and Latin American due to the influence of Manuel Ugarte, Haya de la Torre and APRA.
4. Support for Latin American revolutions in general and the Argentine revolution in particular.
5. An ideological movement of the university middle class in Buenos Aires which later spread to the interior.
6. An anti-imperialist position confronting Great Britain as well as the United States.

---

[11] See Carlos M. Noel, "Política y Económica," *Hechos e Ideas*, I:1 (June, 1935), p. 25; "El gobierno de Entre Ríos," *Hechos e Ideas*, I:2 (July, 1935), 102.

[12] Amadeo Sabattini, "Discurso-programa del Dr. Sabattini," *Hechos e Ideas*, II:5 (November, 1935), pp. 66-69.

[13] *Composición de la Cámara de Diputados*, p. 34.

[14] Arturo Juaretche, *F.O.R.J.A. y la década infame* (Buenos Aires: Editorial Coyoacán, 1962), p. 6.

The Constituent Assembly of FORJA issued two manifestos, the first of which explained the purpose of the organization.[15]

The task of the new emancipation can be realized only by action of the people.
The UCR must be the instrument of this task, completing the work stopped by the overthrow of Hipólito Irigoyen.
In order to do this it is necessary for the party to establish a direct vote of its affiliated members thus assuring popular sovereignty within the party; also it must determine the causes of Argentine enslavement to foreign capital, propose solutions for this, and adopt a method of struggling against the obstacles that oppose the realization of national unity.
It is necessary to struggle within the party so that it can recover the lineage of intransigence that has characterized it since its origin; this is the only way that it can comply with the ideals that gave birth to it.

The second manifesto denounced the Justo government, the National Bank, transportation monopolies, the Roca-Runciman Treaty, petroleum concessions and Argentine participation in the League of Nations. Special condemnation was reserved for the UCR leadership and its at least tacit acceptance of these items.

The members of FORJA were concerned primarily with combating what they thought of as imperialism. They accepted a Marxist interpretation of history, at least as far as the development of capitalism was concerned, but they were searching for a non-Marxist answer to the problem.[16] The closest thing to an answer that they could offer was extensive nationalization of natural resources and abrogation of all treaties which were at all detrimental to the nation's economic welfare or to its political sovereignty.

The record of the Radical congressmen during the last two years of the Justo administration was not particularly illustrious. The voters had given the UCR their enthusiastic endorsement in the 1935 elections, but once again the promised reforms were not forthcoming. Many of UCR congressmen seemed intent only upon gaining their share of the spoils,[17] while others spent their time in useless argu-

---

[15] *Ibid.*, pp. 7-8.

[16] Juaretche [*op. cit.*, pp. 57-58] says "We were not anti-imperialists because of doctrinary reasons—although doctrinary anti-imperialism has been quite useful in the discovery of many truths—but because imperialism opposes the development of our country and the happiness of our people."

[17] See Ysabel Fisk, "Argentina: The Thirteen Year Crisis," *Foreign Affairs*, XXII:2 (January, 1944), p. 263.

ments among themselves. One writer says of the Congress of 1937:[18]

In that year the legislature passed only three laws: one authorized the Chamber to spend more money, and the other two permitted the President to leave the city of Buenos Aires on vacations. Although the executive got its budget to Congress on time, the finance committee did not even get around to meeting until the end of the session. The Conservatives would not attend Congressional sessions, and the Radicals spent their time in interminable minority wrangles. And when the Conservatives were there, the Radicals were absent in protest at fraudulent elections.

As the 1937 UCR National Convention approached, left-wing, anti-imperialist groups were formed within the UCR organizations in several of the provinces. The primary goal of these organizations[19] seems to have been to block the presidential nomination of Alvear, but they were also eager to move the general ideology of the party to the left. Shortly before the convention met there were rumors that the conservative leadership of the UCR was preparing to enter an electoral pact with the Justo government. *País Libre,* the organ of the *Movimiento Ordenador,* announced that such an action "would produce an enormous crisis within the files of the UCR."[20] It also demanded that the approaching convention: (1) nominate only true Radicals, (2) censure the present government, and (3) state the principles of the UCR concisely and without equivocation.[21] The UCR National Committee denied any agreements with the Conservatives, but Lisandro de la Torre claimed that the Radicals had a secret agreement with President Justo whereby they would offer only token opposition to the administration candidate, who in turn was to guarantee free elections and see to it that the UCR succeeded him in power.[22] Although later events lend credibility to De la Torre's accusation, the charge has never been proven. The extreme *Legalistas* who were incensed even at the rumor of a UCR-Conservative *acuerdo* were the ones who rendered impossible a pact with the Socialists and Progressive Democrats. They still retained the messianic *hipolitista* concept of

---

[18] *Ibid.,* p. 262.

[19] The most important of which were *Bloque Opositor* and *Afirmación Radical* in Buenos Aires, *Fuerza Intransigente Radical* in Santa Fe, and *Movimiento Ordenador* in the capital.

[20] Del Mazo, *El Radicalismo,* II, p. 284.

[21] *Ibid.*

[22] Elvira Aldao de Díaz (ed.), *Cartas íntimas de Lisandro de la Torre* (Buenos Aires: Editorial Futuro, 1941), p. 57. See also "La U.C.R. frente a la situación política," *Hechos e Ideas,* IV:13 (July, 1936), pp. 91-92.

the UCR as the elected party, and considered union with other organizations as contamination of the purity of their ideals.

When the UCR National Convention met in April of 1937 it surprised no one by nominating Marcelo T. Alvear as its presidential candidate; the more conservative element of the party was still in control of the national organization. The delegates then proceeded to write the most comprehensive electoral platform in the party's history —the first two and a half pages of which explained why the UCR was not going to boycott the election. Then came a somewhat lengthy statement which was actually a plea to the military to let bygones be bygones. It said, in part:[23]

The National Convention of the UCR declares:
(1) that the UCR as an essentially nationalistic party understands that the armed forces of the republic, which have as their duty the defense of territorial integrity, honor, sovereignty, and the constitution, are necessary institutions within the organization of the state;
(2) that the UCR has sustained, sustains, and will sustain always, the necessity of fortifying the functional efficiency and just prestige of the armed forces and their chiefs and officials who are the depositories of the ideals of American liberty. . . .

The political section of the platform was almost an exact replica of that of 1935, but there were notable additions in the other sections. In the field of economics it advocated the creation of an organization to supervise the production and distribution of most industrial products, nationalization of public services and mines, and the establishment of a maximum legal interest rate. It also advocated a degree of agrarian reform including a strict limitation on the amount of land that might be owned by any single person or family.[24]

The presidential election of 1937 went just as planned by the administration. Roberto Ortiz, the Antipersonalist Minister of Public Works under Alvear and Finance Minister under Justo, was elected through the generous use of force and fraud. The congressional elections of that year must have been somewhat more honestly conducted for the UCR increased its representation in the lower house by 60 per cent, replacing the National Democrats as the largest single party in that Chamber—in fact, if the provincial splinter groups of the party

[23] *Declaración de la Convención Nacional con respecto a las Fuerzas Armadas de la Nación.*
[24] "Resoluciones y Sanciones de la H. Convención Nacional," *Hechos e Ideas,* VI:22 (June, 1937), pp. 113-137.

are counted in the total, 87 of the 158 members of the Chamber were Radicals.[25]

By 1938 the UCR was falling apart. It was badly in need of a leader who could hold the various sectors of the party together, and it became increasingly obvious that Marcelo Alvear was not such a person. He was able to speak only for the more conservative members of the party whose majority was constantly dwindling. The national organization not only had trouble with varying ideologies within it, but it was also unable to control the provincial organizations. In Tucumán the UCR *Concurrencista* was in control, and in Santiago del Estero it was the UCR *Unificada*. In San Juan and Santa Fe the provincial UCR was acting independent of the national organization, and in Catamarca, La Rioja, and Salta, the UCR *Junta Reorganizadora Nacional* was more powerful than the UCR. Even had Alvear been elected to the presidency in 1937, it is doubtful that he could have held the party together.

The next decade in the history of the party was characterized by the organization and disbanding of a great many intraparty factions, most of which were opposed to the UCR's conservative leadership. From about 1938 until the present time it is virtually impossible to speak of "the" UCR position on any given issue. In general, the struggle for control of the party was between the conservative members, led by Alvear until his death in 1942, and the leftist segment which was itself fractionalized until at least 1947. The former group was at first called the *Mayoritarios*, and then after Alvear's death, the Unionists. Indicative of this struggle in 1938 was the conflict within the party in the capital. When the City Convention met in that year two slates of candidates were presented—one representing the Alvearists and the other the Legalists. The former won, but through the use of such fraud that one of the members of the winning slate sent Alvear a telegram renouncing his candidacy in protest of the manner in which he was nominated.[26] Some of the losing candidates decided to run for election on their own as the UCR *Bloque Opositor*. These men were soon removed from the party by the National Committee. Similar events occurred with alarming frequency in other areas of the country.

In May of 1938 the first National Congress of Radical Youth met in Córdoba. The speeches and manifestos of the delegates to this con-

---

[25] *Composición de la Cámara de Diputados*, p. 36.
[26] Felix Luna, *Alvear* (Buenos Aires: Libros Argentinos, 1958), pp. 236-237.

vention and those that followed showed clearly that the younger members of the party were opposed to the conservative Alvearist leadership. The economic principles espoused by this Congress of Radical Youth were considerably to the left of the program of the UCR National Committee. The economic declaration of this Congress said, in part:[27]

We ratify the anti-imperialist position of the UCR, and we demand its complete fulfillment in all the areas of party activity, because we feel that true political liberty cannot exist in this Republic while the economy continues to be subordinated to the interests of international capitalism. . . . We demand the permanent and organic intervention of the state in national economic life in order to impede the advance of privileges and to realize a greater degree of social justice. It is necessary for the state to monopolize public services and to cancel foreign concessions. We adhere to the creation of a petroleum monopoly as sustained during the presidency of doctor Irigoyen. . . .

From this time until the leftist sector of the party gained control of the national organization during the Perón era the various Congresses of Radical Youth attacked the leadership of the UCR. They said that they desired a return to the principles of Irigoyen; in reality they wanted the party to move closer to state socialism in its ideology. They advocated "Immediate and profound agrarian reform"; nationalization of public services, fuels, insurance, and energy resources; and close political and economic ties with the other Latin American nations, in order to combat the imperialists of Washington and London. In general their program was very similar to that of the Peruvian APRA leader, Victor Raúl Haya de la Torre.

Roberto M. Ortiz was elected to the presidency in 1937 in an election typical of those conducted by the Conservative administrations. The general public considered him just another representative of the *estancieros* who would continue the Conservative policy of corruption and repression. However, President Ortiz seems to have thought of himself as another Roque Sáenz Peña, whose duty it was to restore honest elections. In 1938 and 1939 he wrote to several provincial governors demanding that forthcoming elections held in their provinces be conducted honestly and in accordance with the Sáenz Peña Law. In 1939 he annulled the results of a fraudulent election held in San Juan, and he did the same thing in Buenos Aires early the next

---

[27] Del Mazo, *El Radicalismo*, II, pp. 288-289.

year when he removed the fraudulently elected Conservative governor of that important province. And to the horror of the Conservatives, the President saw to it that the congressional elections of 1940 were free of fraud and force. The UCR won about 62 per cent of the contested seats in the Chamber of Deputies, and in the new Congress out-numbered the National Democrats and Antipersonalists combined. The Radicals—and probably the nation as a whole—were hopeful of building a large congressional majority during the next three years and also of winning the presidency in 1943. However, President Ortiz's health deteriorated rapidly in 1940, and by July his near blindness forced him to turn the government over to the Vice-President, Ramón Castillo.[28] The new chief executive immediately reversed the policies of Ortiz; the cabinet was reorganized under arch conservatives and intervention in the provinces assured the return of Conservative domination on the local scene. The Radicals reacted by forcing the Congress to come to a virtual standstill. They even refused to pass a budget.[29]

Only three days after Germany invaded Poland in 1939, President Ortiz announced that he was determined to follow the precedent of Irigoyen and keep Argentina out of World War II. As was the case during World War I the majority of the Argentines were pro-Allies, but they were not at all interested in being dragged into a war taking place thousands of miles away. Besides, the neutrality policy of Irigoyen a quarter of a century earlier had benefited the nation economically, and the populace expected even greater benefits from neutrality during the second war.

As early as October of 1939 Alvear was advocating Argentine aid to the Allies in every manner short of a declaration of war. He did make it clear, however, that Argentina should remain neutral, at least in name.[30] When the UCR National Convention next met, it adopted the same line. Its resolution of March 14, 1941 said:[31]

The UCR manifests its sympathy and its solidarity with the nations that are defending democracy and liberty. . . . We resolve to maintain neutrality in the face of the conflict developing in Europe. . . . We are neutral as a state, neutral from the military point of view, but our neutrality does

---

[28] Ortiz died in 1942 without having reclaimed power.

[29] Ysabel F. Rennie, *The Argentine Republic* (New York: Macmillan, 1945), p. 288.

[30] Marcelo T. Alvear, *Argentinos* (Buenos Aires: M. Gleizer, 1940), pp. 205-212.

[57]

not prevent our manifestations of sympathy for those who struggle for liberty and democracy.

When the United States entered the war, the UCR was willing to alter its policy only slightly. The National Convention of April, 1942, went on record as favoring a rupture of diplomatic relations with the Axis, but it made it quite clear that it was opposed to a declaration of war.

Vice-President Castillo rapidly became one of Argentina's most unpopular executives. Using the bombing of Pearl Harbor as an excuse, he declared a nationwide state of siege in December, 1941; it was never lifted by him. Elections became an absolute farce. For example, the 1942 gubernatorial elections in the province of Tucumán were honest, for some inexplicable reason, and the UCR emerged with a majority of the electoral votes. The Conservative electors refused to attend the electoral college and thus deprived it of a quorum. Instead they wrote to Castillo asking for intervention "to restore electoral normality," which, of course, they had disrupted. The national government quickly intervened and called for new elections.[32]

As the 1943 presidential elections approached, Castillo chose as his successor Robustiano Patrón Costas, a wealthy sugar magnate from Salta. Patrón Costas was not acceptable to anyone, but a sector of the Conservatives; the more liberal parties felt that he would continue the policies of Justo and Castillo, and the pro-Axis part of the population, especially in the armed forces, looked upon him as an extreme Anglophile.

The Socialist Party immediately began efforts to unite with the Progressive Democrats and Radicals in a Democratic Union to oppose the Conservative nominee. The left-wing of the UCR opposed any electoral pact, but they were still in the minority within the party's national organization. The decision was up to the more conservative Unionists. The UCR National Committee agreed to discuss the formation of a Democratic Union after the other two parties agreed that the presidential nominee should be a Radical. Before any real agreement could be reached the armed forces again assumed the role of keeper of the national conscience and deposed President Castillo.

---

[31] Fabian Onsari, *Unidad de los pueblos de América* (Avellaneda, Argentina: [n.p.], 1943), pp. 27-42.

[32] Rennie, *op. cit.*, pp. 300-301.

Chapter V

Radicalism in the Peronist Period: 1943-1955

The 1943 revolution was led by a group of field-grade army officers known as the *Grupo de Oficiales Unidos* or GOU. This organization was formed, after the fall of General Uriburu, to give a political tone to the army. It has often been accused of being fascist; at least it favored an authoritarian government in which the army would have the dominant role. The GOU had no real leader until 1945; for the first two years of its rule there was an obvious power struggle going on within its ranks.[1]

The revolution of June fourth went quite smoothly except for the assumption of the presidency by General Arturo Rawson, who lasted only one day in office. He was succeeded by General Pedro Pablo Ramírez. At first the UCR gave the revolutionary government its "official, frank support."[2] The Radicals were somewhat surprised by the take over by Ramírez on June fifth, but they supported his administration for several months. They seem to have felt that sooner or later they would inherit the revolution—in spite of the fact that there were no Radicals in the government, and Ramírez had not even mentioned elections. By the time Ramírez was replaced by General Edelmiro Farrell in February of 1944, the Radicals had become disillusioned with the revolution, and they finally began to move into the opposition. However, by no means all of the Radicals were willing to follow the party line in this respect. A great many of the members of FORJA joined the revolutionary movement and remained in it even after the resignation of Ramírez.[3]

---

[1] An excellent description of the 1943 revolution and the GOU appear in Ray Josephs, *Argentine Diary* (New York: Random House, 1944).

[2] Josephs, *op. cit.*, p. 17.

[3] Arturo Juaretche, *F.O.R.J.A. y la década infame* (Buenos Aires: Coyoacán, 1962), pp. 117-118.

As early as October, 1943, Juan Perón offered the UCR all the cabinet posts in his government-to-be except for the military positions.[4] The party's National Committee, controlled at that time by the conservative Unionists, declined the offer. One can only speculate as to what the answer would have been had the left-wing of the party controlled the National Committee. It is true that this was the group that frequently spoke out against all interparty pacts, but it was also the group that espoused basically the same program that Perón talked about before his election in 1946. From late 1943 until the 1946 election Perón made a concerted effort to attract members of the UCR to his banner, but with the exception of some of the FORJA members who left the UCR soon after the June fourth revolution, he met with limited success. Early in 1945 the UCR National Committee warned party members that collaboration with Perón would bring expulsion from the party. In spite of this warning, three Radicals—Juan H. Quijano, Armando G. Antille, and Juan I. Cooke—accepted ministerial positions in the Farrell government in 1945. All three were almost immediately read out of the party.

Late in 1945 President Farrell announced that elections would be held the following April; he soon moved up the date to February twenty-fourth. As soon as the elections were announced the Socialists and Communists started trying to line-up all of the nation's traditional parties in a unified opposition to the candidacy of Perón. The UCR at first refused to enter any electoral alliance. On August 28, 1945, the party's National Committee passed a resolution supporting "a harmonious action" with other democratic parties against the revolutionary government, but denying the possibility of "alliances or pacts of an electoral character."[5]

When the UCR National Convention met in December of 1945, the principal issue was whether or not the party should join the Socialists, Communists, and Progressive Democrats in the anti-Perón Democratic Union. In general, the Unionists led by Mario Guido and José Tamborini were in favor of joining but the leftist Intransigents, led by Amadeo Sabattini were opposed to it. The former group still controlled the party's national apparatus as was shown by the vote of

---

[4] *La UCRI, Palanca del Desarrollo Nacional y la Justicia Social: 70 años de luchas políticas del pueblo* (Buenos Aires: Ediciones UCRI, 1961), p. 26.

[5] Santiago Nudelman, *El Radicalismo al servicio de la libertad* (Buenos Aires: Editorial Jus, 1947), pp. 226-227.

115 to 48 in favor of entering the Democratic Union.[6]

The parties of this anti-Perón coalition agreed that the UCR should nominate both the presidential and vice-presidential candidates who would then receive the complete support of the other three parties. The National Democrats (conservatives) declined to enter the Democratic Union formally, but they agreed not to run candidates for executive offices and thus free their members to vote for the Radicals. The UCR nominated José Tamborini and Enrique Mosca—both of whom were ex-Antipersonalists, and among the most conservative of the party's members.

In January, 1946, the ex-Radicals who were supporting the revolutionary government organized as the *Unión Cívica Radical Junta Reorganizadora* and nominated Perón as their presidential candidate. He also received the nomination of the newly formed *Partido Laborista*.

The election itself was conducted quite honestly, but this was of little value to the Democratic Union candidates for the entire campaign was conducted under a state of siege. Tamborini-Mosca rallies were frequently an open invitation to violence which the police usually stood by and watched. If the violence used against the democratic candidates were not enough, Perón bought and wrapped up the election with the issuance of his famous *aguinaldo* [Christmas present] decree;[7] this decree provided for a general salary increase—for all but domestic and public servants—of from 5 to 20 per cent, plus an annual Christmas bonus of one month's pay. It has been estimated that this decree purchased tens of thousands of votes, "probably enough to swing the election."[8] The vehement protests against this decree by businessmen and industrialists—who were supporting Tamborini— must have gained Perón even more votes.

Perón received about 55 per cent of the popular vote and 304 of the 376 electoral votes. *Peronistas* won all the provincial governor-

---

[6] Del Mazo, *El Radicalismo*, III, 62. As soon as this vote was taken, the Intransigents left the Convention and thus the new National Committee chosen was composed entirely of Unionists.

[7] This decree is reprinted in "La política desarrollada por la Secretaría de Trabajo y Previsión: Síntesis completa de la legislación social desde el 4 de junio de 1943 hasta el 4 de junio de 1946," *Hechos e Ideas*, VI:42 (August, 1947), pp. 98-128.

[8] Ruth and Leonard Greenup, *Revolution Before Breakfast* (Chapel Hill: University of North Carolina Press, 1947), p. 146.

ships and control of all the legislatures; they also obtained all the seats in the Senate and two-thirds of the Chamber seats.[9] Two years earlier an American writer had foreseen the plight of the UCR; she said, "The Radical Party . . . has lost its reason for being. It no longer represents any dynamic economic or political interest."[10]

When the results of the 1946 election were made public, the entire National Committee of the UCR resigned. It was later replaced by a seven-man National Executive Council (three Intransigents and four Unionists) which was supposed to suggest a plan for national reorganization of the party. This council accomplished nothing; however the minority report submitted by the three Intransigents pointed out the ever-widening breach within the party. This split came to a head with the formation of the *Movimiento de Intransigencia y Renovación.*

After the 1935 UCR National Convention dropped the abstention policy, various leftist factions were formed within the party.[11] Most of these earlier splinter groups were rather short-lived, but those formed after 1939 gradually coalesced into one organization. Typical of these groups was the *Junta de Reafirmación Radical* founded late in 1939 by Arturo Frondizi, Mario Bernasconi, Alfredo Ribas, and several others. It was anti-Alvear—although not to the extent of some similar organizations—primarily because of his conservatism in economic affairs. Its members were anxious to move the party to the left, and especially wanted the UCR to espouse nationalization of all public services.[12] Quite similar in ideology were the *Movimiento Revisionista* of Buenos Aires and the *Cruzada Renovadora* of Córdoba and the capital; however these two organizations were also in favor of a UCR-led revolution.[13]

Late in 1943 several of the intransigent groups met in an Assembly of Intransigent Radicalism. The delegates, who came from about half the provinces, seemed to be concerned primarily in forming a unified front against the Unionists at the next national convention. They were

---

[9] The UCR did win the elections in Corrientes, but that province was intervened before any of the Radicals could take office. See Bernardo Rabinovitz, *Sucedió en la Argentina: lo que no se dijo* (Buenos Aires: Ediciones Gure, 1956), pp. 70-71.

[10] Ysabel Fisk, "Argentina: The Thirteen Year Crisis," *Foreign Affairs*, XXII:2 (January, 1944), p. 226.

[11] See *supra*, pp. 49-54.

[12] Felix Luna, *Alvear* (Buenos Aires: Libros Argentinos, 1958), p. 256.

[13] Del Mazo, *El Radicalismo*, II, pp. 295-296.

anxious to round up as many votes as possible because of their fear that the Unionists were going to form an alliance with the other democratic parties. The program of this Assembly emphasized electoral abstention, nationalization of public services, provincialization of the territories, and redistribution of land.[14] Jealousy between the various groups represented at this Assembly prevented any great degree of unity of action for another year and a half, but on April 4, 1945, these groups agreed to unite as the *Movimiento de Intransigencia y Renovación*.[15] On that date they issued the so-called Declaration of Avellaneda, which repeated the general program advocated by the Assembly of Intransigent Radicalism, but also included such statements as "land is for whoever works it," and "natural energy, public services, and all monopolies—foreign or domestic—which impede economic progress must be nationalized."[16]

In spite of the general agreement at Avellaneda in 1945 very little was done to organize the MIR for another two years. Then in January of 1947—just before the UCR National Convention was to meet—another General Assembly of the MIR met and chose a committee to draw up plans for a national organization; and, more important, the members present decided not to attend the party's National Convention later that month. Finally, on August 9, 1947, the first National Congress of the MIR met. A great deal of time was devoted to ringing denunciations of the Unionist sector of the party which was characterized as "reactionary." The most important pronouncement issued by the Congress was an eleven-point "Basis of Political Action" which advocated:[17]

(1) Federalism; provincialization of territories[18]
(2) Feminine suffrage; primary elections
(3) Educational reform; equality of opportunity
(4) Economic democracy; an economy controlled by the state for the benefit of all the people
(5) Nationalization of: public services, transportation, fuel, and all foreign monopolies
(6) Freedom for labor organizations
(7) Agrarian reform
(8) Social reform; health protection; social security

---

14 *Ibid.*, pp. 296-300.
15 Henceforth called MIR.
16 Del Mazo, *El Radicalismo*, II, pp. 301-302.
17 *Ibid.*, pp. 325-327.
18 Provinces enjoy a degree of self-government not accorded territories.

(9) Financial reform; restriction of bureaucratic costs

(10) Economic cooperation with Latin America and the rest of the world

(11) A return to the international policy of Irigoyen; no political ties with foreign nations or international organizations

The *hipolitista* strain of the MIR was also seen in its bitter denunciation of pacts between the UCR and other parties; this group was as messianic in its thought as had been Irigoyen.

The groups which formed the MIR had long been characterized by their stand against economic imperialism, but the MIR in 1947 began to sound anticapitalist, using such phrases as "the degenerate capitalists." Most commentators agree that the intransigent wing of the UCR was by 1947 completely socialistic in its ideology. The Unionists claimed that the MIR was more interested in state ownership than in greater production and aid to the consumer, and thus was not composed of real Radicals.[19] However, none of the three acknowledged leaders of the MIR could fairly be called Socialists. They were Moisés Lebensohn, the President of Radical Youth; Gabriel del Mazo, the leader in the struggle for university reform; and Arturo Frondizi, the leader of the largest of the intransigent groups that formed the MIR.

By 1948 the Intransigents, few of whom were still outside the MIR organization, had control of most of the UCR provincial committees. The MIR by this time had its own officers, its own membership list, and was to all intents and purposes a party within a party. In an attempt to forestall an intransigent take-over of the national apparatus of the party, the Unionists set up their own intraparty organization to which they gave the name *Núcleo Unidad*. However, at the 1948 National Convention the left wing of the party gained the upper hand for the first time since the 1931 reorganization. The official statements of the party reflected this change in leadership. For example, the National Committee soon announced that the time had arrived "for the UCR to move to the left."[20] From 1948 until 1957 the Intransigents retained control of the national party organization, although the extent of their majorities at the national conventions fluctuated from year to year.[21]

---

[19] Manuel Augusto A. Gondra, *Declinación del Radicalismo y política del futuro* (Buenos Aires: El Mirador, 1957), pp. 49-51.

[20] *Ibid.*, p. 49.

[21] By far the best discussion of the intransigent sector of the party and the MIR in particular is in Gabriel del Mazo, *El Radicalismo: El Movimiento de Intransgencia y Renovación, 1945-1957* (Buenos Aires: Ediciones Gure, 1957).

In 1948 *Peronista* congressmen brought up a proposal for constitutional reform. They had two fundamental changes in mind: making the president eligible for immediate reelection, and granting him greater power to regulate the nation's economy. The UCR congressmen opposed revision of the 1853 Constitution, supposedly because there was no real need for change, and because the Peronists did not have the votes legally to call a Constitutional Convention.[22] In actuality, they opposed any increase in the powers of President Perón; however, it must be admitted that the UCR had not been willing to allow immediate reelection even of Irigoyen. When the question came to a vote in the Chamber of Deputies, the UCR representatives were absent, in protest against the expulsion of their floor leader Ernesto Sammartino,[23] but their forty-two votes would not have changed anything.

In October of 1948 a special National Convention of the UCR was called to decide upon the party's policy with respect to the election of delegates to the Constitutional Convention and what UCR delegates should do if elected. In general, the Unionists wanted to boycott the elections and emphasize the illegality of the convention and the fact that its primary purpose was legalization of the continuance of the Perón dictatorship. On the other hand, the Intransigents favored the nomination of delegates, who if elected would point out the illegality of the convention and refuse to take part in the debates.[24] When the latter group carried the vote, the Unionists decided not to allow their members to enter the elections, and thus there were no UCR candidates on the ballots in Salta, Jujuy, and La Rioja.[25] The results of the election of delegates to the Constitutional Convention were about the

---

[22] While the *Peronistas* had a monopoly on the Senate seats, in the Chamber they had fewer than two-thirds of the total number of seats (because of deaths and resignations), although they had over two-thirds of the votes at any given time. Article I, Section 30 of the Constitution of 1853 said, "either the whole or any part of this constitution may be amended. The necessity for such amendment must be declared by Congress by a vote of at least two-thirds of its members; but the amendment shall not be made except by a convention summoned for that purpose."

[23] See George I. Blanksten, *Perón's Argentina* (Chicago: University of Chicago Press, 1953), pp. 72-74.

[24] There were at least three other plans presented to the convention: (1) the nomination of delegates who would then refuse to attend the meetings of the convention; (2) the selection of delegates who would attend the convention and defend the 1853 Constitution; and (3) the selection of delegates who would put forth UCR proposals for constitutional revision.

[25] Rabinovitz, *op. cit.*, p. 106. The Socialists, Conservatives, and Progressive Democrats also abstained from voting.

same as those of the 1948 congressional election—109 Peronists and 48 Radicals.

Although the National Convention had decided that the Radical delegates should declare the illegality of the convention and then withdraw, the Intransigents did not follow instructions. They entered into a discussion of Peronist reforms, served on committees, and thus gave their tacit approval to the convention. Only when it became obvious that the Peronist delegates were going to push through changes broadly increasing executive power did the Intransigents walk out.[26] Thus the same group of Radicals who had censured *Mayoritarios* for entering elections and serving in Congress between 1935 and 1943, adopted the same policy once they assumed control of the party. It might be pointed out, however, that the conservative sector of the party entered elections during the "Conservative Era" and later espoused abstention during the Perón period, while the Intransigents wanted nothing to do with the Conservative administrations, but were willing to serve in the Peronist dominated Congress.

When the UCR delegates left the Constitutional Convention during its latter stages, the party announced that it would never recognize the legality of the new Constitution. Soon after this announcement, however, the National Committee decided to allow Radical congressmen to take an oath of allegiance to the new document and thus retain their seats. Needless to say, the Unionists voiced their disapproval of this decision. The decision of the National Committee may have been influenced by the results of the election in Santiago del Estero where the vote for UCR candidates was up from 8,000 to 21,000.[27]

It is somewhat difficult to characterize the legislative work of the UCR during the Perón era, for the Radical congressmen were faced with a *Peronista* majority that controlled over two-thirds of the seats at all times and thus could pass or defeat any bill they desired. This huge *Peronista* majority was also used to expel from Congress the UCR delegates who were too vociferous in their opposition. The gen-

---

[26] The most important changes made by the 1949 Convention were those which greatly increased the powers of the president and made him eligible for immediate reelection. Also direct election of the chief executive and senators was substituted for the former indirect systems, and the term of office for congressmen was changed. Under the 1853 Constitution all deputies and half of the senators were elected every two years. In 1949 the term for all congressmen was extended to six years with half retiring each three years.

[27] *Hispanic American Report*, II:5 (May, 1949), p. 20.

eral tactic of the UCR congressmen was to wait for the *Peronista* introduction of a bill, and then deliver long and frequently vehement speeches against it. The Radicals were frequently accused of opposing all *Peronista* measures even if the UCR program espoused the same thing, and it is true that they seem to have interpreted their role in Congress as that of informing the people of the adverse effects of Peronist laws.

It is not completely true that the UCR offered no positive program of its own in Congress. On the whole the differences between Unionist[28] and Intransigent congressmen were laid aside and the two sectors of the party tried—usually in vain—to obtain passage of a limited number of bills. Primarily, they attempted: (1) to get the national government to sell land to *campesinos* at very low prices, (2) to free trade unions from political control, (3) to protect provincial rights against encroachment by the national government, (4) to nationalize railroads, telephone companies, and all sectors of the petroleum industry, (5) to revise the education code so as to grant a greater degree of university autonomy, and (6) to get Argentina out of the United Nations.[29] The UCR congressmen also did a lot of talking about Latin American unity, but they made no effort to pass legislation in this area.[30]

Many of the critics of the congressional role of the UCR during the Perón period do not give sufficient weight to the difficulties that the Radicals were working under. For example all of the Radical congressmen realized that they were liable to be removed from Congress and imprisoned at any time. In August of 1949, Ernesto Sammartino, the UCR floor leader in the Chamber of Deputies, was deprived of his seat because of his criticism of Perón both in Congress and in the nation's leading newspapers. The vote to expel him was strictly according to party lines, with the UCR minority helpless to aid its leader.[31] In the fight to keep Sammartino from being expelled Ricardo

---

[28] Although they espoused party abstention from elections after 1948, the Unionists ran for and assumed seats in Congress.

[29] See Del Mazo, *El Radicalismo*, II, pp. 334-377.

[30] One of the leaders of the MIR said in 1953, "In order to free ourselves from economic oppression we must integrate ourselves in an economic unity with our neighboring countries. . . . One of the great objectives of the Radical Civic Union is the union of the Latin American nations." [Moisés Lebensohn, *Pensamiento y acción* (Buenos Aires: Talleres Gráficos Buenos Aires, 1956), pp. 206-207.]

[31] As a result of this, all the other Radical congressmen resigned their seats.

Balbín gave several speeches in which he was quite harsh in his criticism of Perón. For this offense he too was expelled, so as to deprive him of his congressional immunity and make him liable to criminal prosecution for "disrespect." After his removal from Congress the government did not seem to be anxious to prosecute him under the *desacato* law; however, when he was nominated for the governorship of Buenos Aires a few months later, the disrespect charge was convenient to keep him out of office. He was arrested on the day of the election, and, after a somewhat lengthy trial, was convicted and sentenced to five years imprisonment. In order to keep him from becoming a UCR martyr, President Perón soon gave him a full pardon.[32]

As the 1951 elections approached the UCR again was embroiled in an intraparty conflict over whether or not to nominate candidates. Prior to the National Convention of that year the Unionists met and decided to fight for abstention; they knew well that the Intransigents favored participation in the election. In 1951 a policy of electoral abstention could hardly have been beneficial to the UCR. The Unionists seem to have ignored the Organic Statute of Political Parties which stated that any party that failed to enter candidates in a national election would automatically be denied the right to engage in any political activity.[33] Thus had the Unionists not been outvoted by the Intransigents at the National Convention the UCR would have been forced to renounce all its seats in Congress and in the provincial legislatures; no longer would it have had a forum from which to speak to the nation with parliamentary immunity (even if this protection was somewhat less than perfect); and the party would have had to disband or risk constant persecution and imprisonment of its members.

For the first time in several years the question of electoral alliances was not an issue at the 1951 Convention. The Organic Statute of Political Parties had made such alliances grounds for the legal dissolution of parties. There was little competition for the presidential and vice-presidential nominations; they went to Ricardo Balbín and Arturo Frondizi. Balbín had become something of a martyr within

However the UCR National Committee convinced them to return to the Chamber and work against constitutional reform.

[32] For a more detailed discussion of the expulsion of Sammartino and Balbín and the imprisonment of the latter, see Rabinovitz, *op. cit.*, pp. 103-122.

[33] Shortly after the passage of this law the UCR National Committee issued a statement (August 6, 1945) which said in effect that the party refused to recognize the validity of the law. (See Nudelman, *op. cit.*, pp. 221-222.)

the party after his imprisonment in 1950 and Frondizi was one of the founders of the MIR who had gained a great deal of publicity as Balbín's attorney during his disrespect trial. The electoral platform was basically that of the MIR with additional sections complaining of the totalitarian nature of the Perón government. Also a new section dealing with foreign policy was added. It said, in part:[34]

The National Convention . . . declares (1) that it repudiates all imperialist maneuvers which are aimed at the political, economic, or military dominance of any nation . . . ; (3) that it reaffirms its will to resist all manifestations of imperialism regardless of the section of the world in which they take place; (4) that, in the name of Argentine sovereignty, it opposes the enforcement of all treaties, in effect or made in the future, which signify any form of political, economic, or military hegemony; (5) that it opposes all conventions or treaties which stain the sentiment of *Argentinidad*, and it proposes a neutral position in all questions alien to the great ideals of our nation and the other nations of Latin America, and it proposes universal peace upon the basis of human solidarity and equality. . . .

When the party platform and program were approved—both by wide margins—the Unionists and a dissident sector from Córdoba walked out of the convention.[35]

Even though Perón did very little campaigning the results of the election were a foregone conclusion; eight years of dictatorship had left their mark on the democratic parties. Perón received about 62 per cent of the popular vote[36]—the 1949 Constitution abolished the electoral college vote—and *Peronistas* won all of the congressional seats except for twelve in the Chamber of Deputies obtained by the UCR. Only in the federal capital did the Radicals obtain a respectable percentage of the vote.

With its congressional representation thus diminished and split into two antagonistic factions the UCR was reduced to almost complete impotence during the last four years of the Perón era. In 1954 when

---

[34] Del Mazo, *El Radicalismo*, III, pp. 171-172.

[35] They were quick to point out that in 1937 when their positions had been reversed the leftist sector of the party walked out.

[36] "La elección del General Perón—cifras de los escrutinios y nomina de los electos," *Hechos e Ideas*, II:92 (November, 1951), pp. 196. The results of the presidential election were:

Perón	(*Partido Peronista*)	4,745,157
Balbín	(*Unión Cívica Radical*)	2,406,050
Pastor	(*Partido Demócrata*)	174,315
R. Ghioldi	(*Comunista*)	71,407
A. Ghioldi	(*Partido Socialista*)	54,916

the National Convention met to nominate a candidate for the vice-presidential election of that year it had some difficulty finding a person to run for that office. The party's standard bearer of 1951, Balbín, refused to accept the nomination, and a man virtually unknown outside the party, Crisólogo Larralde, was chosen. Again Unionists and *sabattinistas* (Radicals of the province of Córdoba), who wanted the UCR to boycott the election, refused to support the party nominee who received slightly less than one-third of the vote.

By 1955 the UCR was at its lowest point in this century. It had lost many of its members to Peronism, and some had left the party to join the Communists; what was left of the party was split to the extent that the minority faction refused to follow the program of the party's national organization.[37] In September of that year the UCR received a new lease on life when the nation's armed forces removed the Peronist dictatorship.

---

[37] As early as 1930 one of the members of the UCR wrote a book to explain the psychological reasons for the numerous party splits [A. Gutiérrez Díaz, *Nuestro Radicalismo* (Buenos Aires: Talleres Gráficos Argentinos, 1930)], and in 1955 Gabriel del Mazo said of the splits and internal dissention within the UCR, "it is the normal state of the party." [*El Radicalismo*, II, p. 28.]

Chapter VI

Two Radical Parties: 1955-1958*

With the Peronist dictatorship gone, the UCR once again became the nation's strongest political force. The only group capable of effective opposition to the Radicals was the *Peronistas*, but the Revolutionary Government almost immediately banned all political activity by this movement.[1] The Socialists, Progressive Democrats and National Democrats were without effective organizations; none of them had elected a congressman since 1948. It was obvious that if the military government allowed free elections, the Radicals would have very little opposition.

When the UCR National Committee met in March, 1956, the intransigent wing of the party was in complete control—there was only one Unionist delegate. The committee chose Arturo Frondizi as its President; his only possible opponent for the position, Ricardo Balbín, cast the first vote for him.[2] The committee was somewhat noncommital in respect to the provisional government of General Pedro Aramburu, applauding the revolution, but at the same time asking Aramburu not to do anything but restore order until elections were held to choose a civilian administration. While the committee as a whole was somewhat cool toward Aramburu and his regime, Balbín made a long speech eulogizing the General and his work.

When delegates were chosen to the UCR National Convention of May, 1956, it became clear that the Radicals were no nearer ideological unity than they had been during the Perón dictatorship. A

---

* Part of this Chapter and Chapter VII appeared in the *Journal of Inter-American Studies*, V:4 (October, 1963), pp. 507-531.

[1] See decree 3855 of November 24, 1955.

[2] Gabriel del Mazo, *El Radicalismo: El Movimiento de Intransigencia y Renovación* (Buenos Aires: Ediciones Gure, 1957), p. 268.

large majority of the delegates to the convention were members of the *Movimiento de Intransigencia y Renovación,* but there were also representatives of the *Movimiento de Intransigencia Nacional* from Córdoba, *Unidad Radical* from Mendoza and the *Núcleo Unidad* of Buenos Aires.[3] The Radicals, who must have realized that they would encounter little effective opposition from the other political parties in the forthcoming elections, seem to have been determined to provide that opposition within their own party. For several years the conflict inside the UCR had been between the rather conservative Unionists and the left-wing Intransigents. By 1956 the latter group was firmly in control of the national party, and the Unionists were strong in only a few provinces. At this time, however, the Intransigents began to argue among themselves; even within the MIR there were antagonistic personalist factions. It would appear that from the fall of Perón until the present time the quarrels among Radicals have been based more upon personalities than on real political or economic issues. With the outlawing of the Peronist party it became apparent that the UCR was going to gain control of the government—but who, or what group, would control the UCR?

On September 24, 1956, Arturo Frondizi announced that he would be the presidential nominee of the UCR in the yet-to-be-called elections. This announcement caused quite a stir within the party, for the National Convention which was to nominate candidates was not scheduled to meet until November ninth. There were rumors of the formation of a second National Committee to oppose the one controlled by Frondizi, but nothing was done at this time. When the convention was held, Frondizi was unopposed for the presidential nomination. It must be pointed out, however, that of the convention's 204 delegates, 42 refused to attend the meetings and another 28 attended but refused to vote.[4] The convention did not write an electoral platform, but instead sanctioned the one written in 1951 and used again in 1954 (which was, on the whole, the 1945 Declaration of Avellaneda). The delegates also issued a statement demanding that general elections be held before there was any attempt at constitutional reform. They pointed out that constitutional conventions could legally be called

---

[3] Other UCR factions included the *Movimiento de Intransigencia Popular, Movimiento Unificador de la UCR, Movimiento Pro Radicalismo Unido* and *Cruzada Renovadora de la UCR.*

[4] Del Mazo, *op. cit.,* p. 227.

[72]

only by Congress—and in 1956 there was no Congress. One of the major reasons for demanding general elections prior to the convoking of a constituent assembly was that the Radicals were sure that they would win the elections and thus be in a more powerful position when —and if—the constitutional convention were held. On the other hand, the provisional government, which had annulled the 1949 Constitution and reinstated the 1853 document by decree, insisted that delegates to the constitutional convention might desire changes in the system of elections, and thus these changes should be made prior to the general elections themselves.[5]

Almost as soon as Frondizi received the presidential nomination, many of the provincial committees of the UCR called upon him to renounce his candidacy and submit to a direct primary of all party members.[6] During the first three months of 1957, there was wholesale feuding among the various sectors of the UCR. Throughout January of that year, the leaders of the *Núcleo Unidad* tried to find a system of reorganization that would unify the party behind a single presidential candidate, presumably not Frondizi. At the same time the *frondizista* National Committee was also looking for party reorganization, but on altogether different terms from those suggested by the Unionists. The National Committee seems to have been interested primarily in enlisting the membership, or at least the support, of the Peronists who were not allowed to run their own candidates in elections. These overtures to Peronists further intensified the struggle of some of the provincial committees against the national one. On January nineteenth, the leaders of the *Movimiento de Intransigencia Popular* in the capital were removed from the party organization by the city committee.[7] This just accentuated the feud. The National Committee intervened in several of the provincial committees to see to it that Frondizi men were in control of the local organizations, and at the same time many of the provincial committees announced that they no longer recognized the power or jurisdiction of the national organization.[8]

---

[5] Aramburu let it be known that he preferred to see the Sáenz Peña Law amended constitutionally, in order to provide for a system of proportional representation.

[6] Frondizi and the other Intransigents had demanded such a primary when they were in a minority at the National Conventions.

[7] *La Prensa*, January 20, 1957, p. 3.

[8] *Ibid.*, January 31, 1957, p. 1; February 1, 1957, p. 5; and February 7, 1957, p. 3.

The *frondizistas* received a sharp setback on January twenty-fifth when Ricardo Balbín resigned from the National Committee. When the committee met the next day, the delegates, who were members of the Buenos Aires branch of the MIR and the Córdoba MIN, refused to attend. These groups announced their loyalty to Balbín and Amadeo Sabattini, respectively.[9] When the remaining members of the National Committee voiced criticism of the Aramburu government—staunchly supported by Balbín and Sabattini—they further decreased the chances of party reconciliation.

On February ninth, leaders of the various groups hostile to the leadership of the National Committee met in the capital in an attempt to coordinate their actions.[10] Those present included Balbín; Sabattini; Miguel Angel Zavala Ortiz, leader of *Núcleo Unidad;* Santiago Nudelman, leader of the *Movimiento Pro Radicalismo Unido;* and Crisólogo Larralde, UCR vice-presidential candidate in 1954, and possibly the most influential politician in the province of Buenos Aires. After a series of meetings it was announced on February twelfth that the MIR, MIN and *Núcleo Unidad* had agreed to unite as the *Junta Nacional Reorganizadora de la Unión Cívica Radical.*[11] The leaders of the new organization announced that they were forming a second UCR on a national scale. Their first act was the selection of a National Committee headed by Larralde. For about a month there were two UCR National Committees. In order to differentiate between them the Buenos Aires press called the Frondizi group the *Comité Nacional* and the other the *Comité Nacional Provisional.*

On February seventeenth, Larralde gave a nationwide radio address which was supposed to tell the Argentine people the program of the provisional UCR. According to him the new group favored total reorganization of the party, a direct vote in the selection of nominees for public office, defense of the principles of the 1955 revolution, maintenance of the international policy of Irigoyen, and no foreign concessions for the development of natural resources.[12] It seems likely that the *frondizista* group would have agreed with all of these ideas except one—the direct vote for the selection of party nominees. They opposed this

---

[9] *Ibid.*, January 28, 1957, p. 5.

[10] *Ibid.*, February 9, 1957, p. 3.

[11] *Ibid.*, February 13, 1957, p. 3. The next day the MIP and MPRU agreed to join the organization.

[12] *Ibid.*, February 18, 1957, p. 4.

because it might well have cost Frondizi the presidential nomination that he had worked so hard to attain. The anti-Frondizi group favored it for exactly the same reason. The fundamental issue, then, between the two groups was simply should Frondizi be the UCR presidential candidate or should the nomination be given to someone else. It is virtually a certainty that the various sectors of the UCR were anxious to get one of their members in the *Casa Rosada* in order to obtain a greater share of the spoils of office. The lack of ideological differences between the provisional UCR and the Frondizi Radicals was pointed out when the former group gave its enthusiastic endorsement to the 1951-1954 electoral platform which had also been adopted by the *frondizista* delegates to the 1956 National Convention.[13]

During the first two weeks of March there was a great deal of quarreling over the names of the two UCR groups. Each was anxious to gain a legal monopoly on the term *Unión Cívica Radical* for use on the ballots in coming elections. On March nineteenth, the Frondizi faction decided to add the word Intransigent to the party name and thus became the *Unión Cívica Radical Intransigente*.[14] The other faction denounced this action, stating that several of its component groups already had the word Intransigent in their names. They finally acquiesced, however, and a week later announced that they had adopted the title *Unión Cívica Radical del Pueblo*.[15]

The first test of strength for the two new Radical parties came in July, 1957, with the selection of delegates to a Constitutional Convention. Neither party had consolidated its internal organization nor set up comprehensive programs that would allow the voters to differentiate between them. At this time the main issue was whether or not the 1853 Constitution should be amended, or at least, whether or not it should be amended at this time. The *frondizistas*, who had always opposed constitutional reform prior to the holding of general elections, entered candidates with the understanding that those elected would refuse to attend the sessions of the convention. The UCRP candidates were pledged to moderate constitutional reform, especially modernization, but there was some dissention within the party on this point. The MIN wanted to hold a plebiscite first to determine whether the people actually desired changes in the constitution. Failing in this, its

---

[13] *Ibid.*, February 19, 1957, p. 4.
[14] Henceforth called UCRI.
[15] Henceforth called UCRP.

members then suggested that the Constitutional Convention serve as a temporary legislature and choose an acting president.[16] This plan also lacked popular support.

The results of the election of delegates were as follows:

Party	Votes	Per Cent	Delegates
UCRP	2,106,524	24.2	75
UCRI	1,847,603	21.3	77
Socialists	525,721	6.0	12
Christian Democrats	420,606	4.8	9
Democrats	333,749	3.8	9
Progressive Democrats	263,805	3.0	5
Communists	228,821	2.6	2
Other parties	860,632	10.0	7
Blank ballots	2,115,861	24.3	—
Total	8,703,322	100.0	196

Since proportional representation was used in this election, the fact that the UCRI received two more delegates than the URCP was not as important an indication of future strength as the fact that the latter received a plurality of about 260,000 votes. The Popular Radicals had some cause for rejoicing for the same distribution of the vote in general elections would give them the presidency and about 100 of the 187 seats in the lower house of Congress. What the UCRP apparently failed to take into consideration was that its victory had been made possible by the blank ballots cast by Peronists.

When the Constitutional Convention met in September, 77 UCRI delegates and 5 others elected on an antireform platform presented their credentials and immediately walked out. The 19 MIN delegates also threatened to leave if the convention attempted to do anything other than legalize the return to the 1853 Constitution. Had they done so, the convention would immediately have been without a quorum; however, only nine of them left when the delegates began to discuss possible amendments. One of the first important issues to come up was the system of elections. As might have been expected, the delegates who represented the nation's smaller parties (Socialists, Christian Democrats, Progressive Democrats, Conservatives, etc.) favored the adoption of proportional representation. With the division of Radicalism into two large parties it was apparent that minor parties would receive very little representation under the incomplete list system. This was made abundantly clear by the election of delegates to the convention itself. Through the

---

[16] See *Hispanic American Report*, X:4 (April, 1957), p. 205.

use of the d'Hondt form of proportional representation minor parties had obtained 44 delegates; had the incomplete list been used they would have received about five seats. The members of the UCRP, who were in complete control of the convention, were opposed to any change in the Sáenz Peña Law. They had obtained 75 seats through the use of proportional representation, whereas use of the incomplete list would have resulted in 109 UCRP delegates.

As a result of disagreement within the ranks of the UCRP the Constitutional Convention was able to accomplish very little. Constitutional provisions pertaining to civil rights were modernized, but no other fundamental changes were made. Early in October, eleven of the minor party delegates walked out and the convention was forced to adjourn for lack of a quorum.

*　　*　　*

With Peronist parties outlawed as the general elections of February 23, 1958, approached, it was apparent that the new president would come from one of the Radical parties. This was the time for the UCRI and UCRP to adopt positive programs and show the voters the differences in their ideological positions. They did not do so. As was mentioned earlier, both parties declared their adherance to the UCR programs of 1951 and 1954.

The general program of the UCRI was somewhat easier to determine than that of the UCRP, for the former had one acknowledged leader—Arturo Frondizi. The party was formed to a great degree around the personality of this one man. His virtually absolute control of the party might be compared to that of Hipólito Irigoyen between 1900 and 1922. Thus, one would not be far afield if one assumed that the program of the UCRI was that of Arturo Frondizi.

The leader of the UCRI was born in 1908 of a poor family in Corrientes. Shortly after his graduation from law school, he was jailed for his vociferous opposition to the 1930 revolution. Upon his release he joined the UCR where he soon attained a degree of prominence in the *Legalista* sector of the party. In 1935 Frondizi was one of the most vocal of those who opposed dropping of the abstention policy; he did not run for office himself until 1946. He was one of the founders of the *Movimiento Ordenador* in 1937, and gained some national recognition as the editor of *País Libre*, the official organ of that group. His articles in this paper were quite reminiscent of Irigoyen in their messianic appeal. For example, he once wrote, "we do not tell the people

[77]

that we ought to govern because we are the majority, but because our ideals will bring about the renovation of the nation."[17] Frondizi was also influential in the formation of other short-lived intransigent groups, the most notable of which was the *Junta de Reafirmación Radical*. Finally in 1945, with the founding of the MIR, he had a powerful organization within which his ideas could be put into action.

After the revolution in 1943 and the Intransigent take over of the UCR a few years later, Frondizi's ideas on political action did an about-face. During the period of Conservative rule he opposed UCR participation in elections and refused to run for office himself. But during the Perón era he espoused electoral participation on the part of the Radicals and was himself elected to the Chamber of Deputies in 1946. As a member of Congress he was critical of Perón, but this criticism was primarily of the means used by the dictator and not of the basic goal of social and economic reform. He was quite in agreement with the nationalistic position of the Perón government during its early years, but in 1955 when the administration announced a petroleum concession to Standard Oil, he became one of its most bitter critics.

The major part of Frondizi's political philosophy may be found in a book he wrote in 1954, *Petróleo y Política*. A clue to its contents can be found in its subtitle and the title of the introduction which are, respectively: "A Contribution to the Study of Argentine Economic History and the Relationship of Imperialism to National Political Life," and "The Anti-imperialist Struggle as the Fundamental Stage of Democratic Development in Latin America." Frondizi accepts the Marxist thesis that imperialism is a necessary result of ever-expanding capitalism, and he has a tendency to blame on imperialists almost everything which he considers bad. For example, he assigns a major share of the blame for the 1930 revolution to foreign oil companies who wanted to get rid of Irigoyen so that they could regain control of Argentina's vast petroleum reserves.[18] Frondizi[19] makes it clear that his interpretation of history is not completely Marxist—as many of his political opponents claim—when he says, "Human history is not just the history of economics. Man and society are not moved solely by

---

[17] Quoted in Del Mazo, *op. cit.*, p. 284.

[18] Arturo Frondizi, *Petróleo y política* (Buenos Aires: Editorial Raigal, 1954). pp. 271-277.

[19] *Ibid.*, p. iii.

economic facts, but by a conjunction of factors of a different order (spiritual, political, social)."

According to Frondizi, there should be three elements in the socio-economic revolution that he felt was necessary to bring Argentina into the community of world powers. The first was agrarian reform —"without agrarian reform there is no possibility of solving our economic problems."[20] He was somewhat hesitant as to the shape this reform should take. On the one hand, he felt that "it is necessary to give access to the land immediately to whoever works it,"[21] yet he was worried about the inefficiency of a multitude of very small farms. He seemingly would have preferred large cooperatives which should greatly increase production, but he did not want them forced upon the populace. The second step was to be industrialization. This, he thought, was the only way Argentina could defeat the designs of the imperialist nations which were trying to keep the country a producer of raw materials and a market for their industrial products. Frondizi talked a great deal about economic cooperation among all Latin American nations in simultaneous development and industrialization. He believed that with sufficient planning and cooperation the continent could become virtually self-sufficient, and thus deliver itself from the clutches of foreign imperialists.[22] In this industrialization phase the government was to play an important role. He would have the state direct and/or regulate the nation's economy in whatever way was necessary. The third step Frondizi termed "democratization of the economy." He would have immediate nationalization, with just compensation, of all the nation's public services and all monopolies, foreign or domestic. Except for these two areas, however, Frondizi did not favor indiscriminate nationalization. He said it should be undertaken only if it would assure better services or greater production, for "nationalization is not a panacea."[23] In general, the economic program advocated by Frondizi prior to 1958 was quite similar to that of Haya de la Torre, the Peruvian *Aprista* leader, whom he once referred to as the number one citizen of America.

---

[20] Arturo Frondizi, "Algunos aspectos del pensamiento económico radical," *Definiciones Radicales* (La Plata: Comité de la Provincia de Buenos Aires de la UCR, 1955), p. 70.

[21] Frondizi, *Petróleo y política*, p. lxvii.

[22] Arturo Frondizi, *Argentina y América Latina* (Buenos Aires: Presidencia de la Nación, 1958), pp. 11-27.

[23] Frondizi, *Petróleo y política*, p. lxi.

[79]

In the realm of international relations Frondizi espoused the adoption of the program of Irigoyen. He opposed all forms of multilateral agreements, and especially those which might impinge upon Argentina's complete freedom to decide its own foreign policy. He was especially critical of the Pact of Rio de Janeiro which provided that an attack on one American state would be considered an attack on all.[24]

While the general program of the UCRI can be obtained from an examination of the speeches and writings of its leader, this procedure cannot be applied to the UCRP. About the only conclusion that one can reach is that the Popular Radicals had no real platform prior to the 1958 elections. They ratified the UCR program of 1951-1954, but so did the UCRI. The UCRP was greatly handicapped by its heterogeneous composition and by its lack of a clear party leader. The party was, for the most part, composed of all the sectors of the old UCR which were opposed to Frondizi or his National Committee. Even within the three main components of the party there was wide divergence in ideology. The members of the MIN and MIR had more in common with the UCRI than with the Unionists within their own party. The members of the latter group were by far the most conservative of all the Radical factions, and seem to have had only one thing in common with the other segments of the UCRP—opposition to Frondizi.

The Popular Radicals were also handicapped by the lack of clearcut leadership within the party. In spite of the fact that Crisólogo Larralde was President of the party's National Committee, Balbín, Zavala Ortiz and Sabattini all seem to have considered themselves as *the* leader of the party for the first several months of its existence. Even after Balbín received the UCRP presidential nomination, Sabattini and Zavala Ortiz retained the leadership of the MIN and *Núcleo Unidad*. This certainly was not to the advantage of the national party.[25]

---

[24] See Arturo Frondizi, *El tratado de Río de Janeiro* (Buenos Aires: Editorial Denbigh, 1950), pp. 22-45.

[25] About the closest Balbín came to identifying his ideological position during the campaign was a speech of February 15, 1958, when he defined his party as "the struggle against capitalist monopolies and all forms of privilege; agrarian reform; popular education; anti-imperalism; university reform; defense of the economic rights of workers; right of union organization; social security, justice and liberty in all their forms; and defense of national sovereignty." (*La Nación*, February 16, 1958, p. 3.)

At the time of the party split it was generally assumed that the Intransigent Radicals were the former left wing of the UCR, the personal followers of Frondizi, and those who were quite opposed to the administration of General Aramburu. On the other hand, it was felt that the Popular Radicals came from the more moderate sector of the UCR, those who opposed the presidential nomination of Frondizi and who were for the most part quite anti-Peronist. The pro-Aramburu position of the UCRP earned it the title of "Official Party" while its members were labeled by opponents as *continuistas*.

❋   ❋   ❋

As the 1958 elections approached, several parties nominated presidential candidates; however, all of them must have realized that the new president was going to be either Arturo Frondizi or Ricardo Balbín. Early in the campaign Balbín must have been the favorite since his party had outpolled Frondizi's by about 260,000 votes a year earlier. However, in 1957 Peronists had protested by casting blank ballots, the number of which showed that they would hold balance of power in future elections. If they again cast blank ballots the UCRP could probably again come out on top; Peronist support for one of the nation's minor parties would give that party an excellent chance for victory; and Peronist support of one of the Radical parties would almost certainly lead to a clean sweep of the elections. Since the anti-Peronist provisional government of Aramburu had been supported by the Popular Radicals and most of the minor parties, only the anti-Aramburu UCRI and Popular Conservative Party were in a position to campaign effectively for the Peronist vote.

Arturo Frondizi had been doing just this since 1956. He received a great deal of aid from Rogelio Frigerio and his magazine *Qué*. This periodical was able to serve as an outlet for Frondizi's appeal for Peronist support while not being tied officially to either the candidate or his party. From the first of May until the day of the elections *Qué* stressed the economic program of Frondizi and its similarities to the general goals of the Peronist movement. Such as this prompted one Peronist leader to say of the UCRI: "Its discourses, its pronouncements, its postulates, its declarations, its watch-words, sustained and even repeated, in essence, the principles of our doctrine."[26] This author

---

[26] Ricardo C. Guardo, *Horas Difíciles* (Buenos Aires: A. Peña Lillo, 1963), p. 97.

claims that Frondizi met several times with Peronist leaders to explain his program and show how it was basically the program of Peronism.[27] While there is no proof of direct contact between Frondizi and Peronist leaders, it is well known that UCRI leaders and personal friends of Frondizi were in constant contact with Peronists within the country and those in exile in Chile, Uruguay, and Venezuela. Some of these men also visited Perón in Caracas.

One of those making such a trip was Rogelio Frigerio. Many claim that he took with him a copy of an agreement, signed in advance by Frondizi, whose terms included a promise by the UCRI candidate to legalize the Peronist Party in return for the electoral support of that movement in the February twenty-third elections. Frondizi has constantly denied that such an agreement was made; however, shortly before the elections Perón sent word to Argentina that all his followers should vote for UCRI candidates—a gift of approximately two million votes.[28]

Frondizi also received support from other quarters. In January, Mario Amadeo asked the members of his *Unión Federal* to vote for Frondizi;[29] this party had received almost 160,000 votes in 1957. A few days later the head of the Communist Party, Rodolfo Ghioldi, made a speech in which he told all Argentine Communists to vote for the UCRI presidential nominee.[30] Thus Frondizi was handed an additional 250,000 votes from this party. While it is virtually impossible to ascertain exactly how many Peronist, Communist and Federal Union votes Frondizi and the UCRI received, the number must have been quite large.

Frondizi carried the capital and every province, gaining 319 electoral votes to 147 for Balbín. The UCRI won all of the gubernatorial races and control of every provincial legislature; Intransigent Radicals obtained 133 of the 187 seats in the Chamber of Deputies and all the senatorial posts.

---

[27] *Ibid.*, p. 98.

[28] The UCRI had had a distinct advantage in the campaign for Peronist support. The casting of blank ballots, by Peronists would have contributed to victory for Balbín and the UCRP, who represented—to Peronists—a continuance of the hated policies of Aramburu. Support of Vicente Solano Lima, the Popular Conservative leader, might well have led to his victory, but in spite of his anti-Aramburu stand Lima was still a Conservative. Support of Frondizi guaranteed his victory and the possible implementation of a program not far removed from Peronism.

[29] See the *Hispanic American Report*, XX:1 (January, 1958), p. 44.

[30] *La Nación*, February 1, 1958, p. 6.

The vote for President and members of the Chamber of Deputies was divided in the following manner:

Party	President		Deputies	
	Votes	Per Cent	Votes	Per Cent
UCRI	4,070,875	44.9	3,761,248	41.5
UCRP	2,618,058	28.9	2,299,291	25.4
Other parties	1,536,322	16.9	2,345,055	25.5
Blank ballots	838,243	9.3	759,461	7.6
Total	9,063,498	100.0	9,065,055	100.0

Chapter VII

The Frondizi Administration: 1958-1962

After his inauguration Frondizi acted in a manner almost diametrically opposed to his former writings and speeches. Illustrative of this was his Stabilization and Development Program. For several years Argentina had endured the effects of rampant inflation and an extremely unfavorable balance of trade and payments; by 1958 the entire economy was virtually in ruins, due largely to the financial policies of the Perón and Aramburu administrations. In order to combat this situation a Stabilization and Development Program was put into effect on January 1, 1959. The general aims of the program were threefold: (1) curb inflation, (2) create financial stability through austerity, and (3) increase production and thus raise the standard of living. On the first day of 1959, most government subsidies and price controls were dropped, credit was severely tightened, and multiple exchange rates were discontinued. At the same time the government announced that all future wage increases would be limited to corresponding increases in productivity. The greatest burden of the program fell upon the nation's wage earners whose capacity to consume was drastically reduced in 1959 and 1960. On the other hand the property owners and entrepreneurs apparently received an even higher percentage of the gross national product than they had in 1958.[1]

A large part of Frondizi's economic program was dependent upon his ability to make the country self-sufficient in petroleum products. One of the major causes of Argentina's unfavorable balance of trade was the necessity to import well over half its fuel needs. In fact, by 1958 the cost of petroleum imports was almost equal to the deficit in

---

[1] See Robert A. Potash, "Argentina's Quest for Stability," *Current History*, XLII:246 (February, 1962), p. 74.

the balance of payments. Frondizi decided early in his term that foreign capital was essential to the rapid exploitation of the nation's own petroleum resources. The granting of foreign concessions, however, was quite a risky venture, because the state oil monopoly had long been the symbol of economic nationalism in Argentina—in spite of the fact that it had never been able to meet the nation's need for petroleum products. As early as July, 1958, the President signed contracts with Belgian Petrofina and United States Panamerican International for the exploration, drilling and transportation of oil for YPF. When the contracts were announced, Frondizi stressed the fact that the foreign companies were to be paid in cash and not oil, and that YPF would still own the oil in the ground and market what was produced by the foreign companies. Still there was an obvious contradiction between the position he had taken in *Petróleo y política* and the granting of foreign concessions. In 1954 foreign oil companies operating in Argentina were condemned as imperialists who threatened the nation's sovereignty. Four years later it was assumed that the absence of foreign companies posed exactly the same danger. In a radio address of July 24, 1958, Frondizi said:[2]

The principle obstacle to the advance of the country is its dependence upon the importation of fuel. This dependence weakens our capacity for self-determination and places our sovereignty in danger.

In his inaugural speech the President had alluded to the possibility of agreements such as those negotiated with the foreign oil companies, saying "We will accept the cooperation of private capital when official resources are insufficient, but without granting concessions or renouncing the state monopoly on natural resources."[3] As might have been expected, these agreements were criticised by the opposition, especially the UCRP, as "a sell-out to foreign imperialism." To buttress this accusation, Frondizi's own writings were quoted at length.

The about-face in petroleum policy is by no means the only area in which there were fundamental differences between Frondizi's campaign platform and his actions after taking office. In general, candidate Frondizi talked about statist solutions to economic problems, re-

---

[2] "La Batalla del Petróleo" reprinted in Arturo Frondizi, *Política Económica Nacional* (Buenos Aires: Arayú, 1963), p. 93.

[3] Message to Congress of May 1, 1958, reprinted as "Hora Cero de un Nuevo Gobierno" in *Política Económica Nacional*, p. 65.

taining the status quo in religious questions, a nationalistic program in regard to the development of natural resources, and greater freedom of union activities. On the other hand, President Frondizi championed free enterprise, forced a bill through Congress allowing the establishment of Catholic universities, granted oil concessions to foreign companies and broke strikes through the use of the army and a state of siege. Why was there such a difference between the writings and speeches of the candidate and the actions of the President? One observer would answer the question in the following manner:[4]

Frondizi could not have been elected had he not been willing to accept support from any available source, and he also could not have been elected had he shattered his own party by saying openly what he intended to do. In short, the price of his victory was that he had to bed himself with any strange fellow who happened along, and that he had to disguise his intentions even to his legitimate bedmates. . . . Falsehoods and grotesque coalitions were required for victory.

There is probably a degree of truth in this; however, while it might explain the discrepancies between his campaign speeches and his actions after taking office, it does not take into account the fact that Frondizi's campaign promises were not at all new to his political philosophy. During the 1958 campaign he simply reiterated what he had been saying for the past quarter century.

In March of 1962 Frondizi attempted to explain this apparent contradiction in this manner:[5]

I have never accepted the Declaration of Avellaneda [the 1945 program of the MIR which formed the basis of the UCRI platform in 1958] in its entirety. . . . When Perón fell in 1955, thus opening the possibility that we [the UCR] could gain power, examination of concrete problems made it apparent that the Declaration of Avellaneda could not serve as a blueprint for the transformation of the country. . . . That document is concerned with the democratization of industry while our current problem is the creation of that industry.

In the specific instance of petroleum policy Frondizi said that his goal had always been national self-sufficiency, and the preferred means a state monopoly; once the means were shown to be impracti-

---

[4] K. H. Silvert, "Economics, Democracy and Honesty: An Assessment of the Frondizi Regime," *American University Field Staff Reports,* VII:1 (April 10, 1960), p. 10.

[5] Felix Luna, *Dialogos con Frondizi* (Buenos Aires: Desarrollo, 1963), pp. 50, 52, 65.

cable they were changed, but the end remained the same.[6]

It would appear, to this writer at least, that Frondizi's pronouncements prior to 1958 reflected his true political ideology—not just the hypocrisy of a politician looking for votes—and that upon gaining office he realized the impracticability of this philosophy.[7] While he may have sounded like an idealist prior to his election, after that time he assumed the role of a quite astute politician.

✻　　✻　　✻

The heterogeneous coalition which put Frondizi and the UCRI in office would have been difficult to hold together under the best of conditions, and the policies of the new President removed any chance of this. The 1955 decree dissolving the Peronist Party was converted to law by the UCRI Congress in November of 1958; three months later Frondizi interpreted the law to prohibit the nomination of candidates by neo-Peronist parties in the provincial elections of March, 1959. Thus when the people of Catamarca, San Luis and Corrientes went to the polls to choose local officials they were confronted with a situation analagous to that of February, 1958. However, instead of again backing UCRI candidates, Peronists returned to their 1957 technique of casting blank ballots. Intransigent Radicals came out on top in all three provinces, but by the narrowest of margins. Rather than risk defeat in the populous province of Santa Fe, Frondizi postponed elections there for four months. When the elections finally were held victory went to the UCRP; and even the number of blank ballots exceeded those obtained by Intransigent Radicals. These provincial elections showed that the UCRI represented, at most, a quarter of the electorate.

Popular dissatisfaction with his administration as demonstrated at the polls was only one of many problems to face President Frondizi during the first months of his term. Peronists, convinced that support of the UCRI had gained them little (the Party was still illegal and their unions still under intervention), turned to violence. Within six months of his inauguration Frondizi was confronted with a wave of Peronist-led strikes which in some instances were quite violent. In November he was forced to resort to the application of a state of siege

---

[6] *Ibid.*, pp. 51-52, 67.

[7] The possibility certainly exists that Frondizi had changed his mind about certain programs prior to his actual election, but felt compelled to remain silent about them for the time being.

to stay in control of the situation. As the tempo of violence increased the army had to be used. In return for its aid the military demanded the dismissal of Rogelio Frigerio, who was serving as the President's Secretary for Socioeconomic Affairs. This was probably the beginning of a gradual transfer of power from the President to the leaders of the nation's armed forces.

On November thirteenth it was announced that the Vice-President, Alejandro Gómez, was involved in the preparation of a coup d'etat. The Minister of Interior, Alfredo Vítolo, claimed that Gómez had demanded that the President resign or assume the responsibility for virtual civil war. Gómez denied this, claiming that Vítolo and Frigerio were plotting against him. The UCRI immediately removed the Vice-President from the party and demanded that he resign from the government. He refused to do so, and dared the Congress to impeach him. No proof of Gómez complicity in the plotting of a coup was ever offered and the Argentine press soon began to show doubts about the charges. On November seventeenth he was readmitted to the UCRI, and Frondizi publicly cleared him of any wrong-doing. However, the President still asked for his resignation because of policy disagreements. The next day Gómez officially resigned. By this time the affair had begun to look like a comic opera; it did little to enhance the prestige of either the President or his party.

Throughout 1959 Frondizi was confronted with general strikes, mob violence, and attempted coups on the part of Peronists, Communists, and members of the armed forces. To add to his problems, in June of that year Perón released to the press photostats of a document purported to be the pact signed in 1958 by himself, Frigerio, and Frondizi. This further angered military leaders who, according to some, would have deposed the President at this time had there been a vice-president to succeed him constitutionally.[8] Frondizi managed to placate the armed forces, for the time being, by removing from office all persons in any way connected with Communism, Peronism or "Frigerioism."

As the 1960 congressional elections approached the government announced that neither Peronists nor Communists would be allowed to nominate candidates. Any hopes on the part of the administration that these groups would again support the UCRI were dashed when

---

[8] After Gómez resignation Frondizi refused to call a special election to fill the vacancy.

both decided to protest their illegality by means of blank ballots. During the campaign Intransigent Radicals were rather quiet. While the economic program pursued by Frondizi was probably essential, it was not the sort of thing designed to gain electoral support from the middle and lower classes. UCRI candidates tried to explain the long-term benefits that would come from the Stabilization and Development Program, but it seems doubtful that such could sway the votes of those whose incomes had remained relatively steady in the face of rapidly increasing prices. The UCRP attacked the administration at every possibility. It denounced the petroleum concessions as a "sell-out to foreign imperialism," claimed that Frondizi was allowing the International Monetary Fund to dictate the nation's financial policy, and labeled intervention in trade unions "a return to Peronism."

The results of the March twenty-seventh elections were interpreted as a resounding defeat for both President Frondizi and the Intransigent Radicals. The UCRI lost 22 seats in the Chamber of Deputies, and managed to retain its majority in that house only because 66 of its members were not up for election. On the other hand, the UCRP gained 25 Chamber seats while outpolling its principle opponent by almost 287,000 votes. While the vote for Popular Radicals was down about 8 per cent from 1958, the UCRI vote was down approximately 44 per cent. A comparison of the vote obtained by major parties in 1957, 1958 and 1960 shows how dependent the UCRI was upon Peronist votes for its 1958 triumphs.

Party	1957	1958	1960
UCRI	1,847,603	3,761,248	1,832,248
UCRP	2,106,524	2,299,291	2,119,094
Minor parties	2,633,334	2,345,255	2,732,688
Blank ballots	2,115,861	759,461	2,228,014
Total vote	8,703,322	9,065,055	8,912,044

While the press in the United States generally attributed the UCRI losses to popular dissatisfaction with the administration's economic policy, a comparison of the results of the 1957, 1958, and 1960 elections would seem to show that about all that happened in 1960 was the withdrawal of Peronist and Communist votes from the UCRI. In the elections of 1957 and 1960 the percentage of the total vote obtained by each of the Radical parties, the minor parties (taken as a unit), and the blank ballots in no case varied by as much as 0.7 per cent. It would thus appear that the UCRI vote was abnormally high

[89]

in 1958 almost solely due to the support given that party by Peronists, Communists, and members of smaller parties, and that in 1960 the vote obtained by Intransigent Radicals merely returned to its normal level.

Whether or not Frondizi interpreted the results of the 1960 elections as a public repudiation of his economic policies he did not waver in his conviction that the Stabilization and Development Program must be continued. Just six months after the election, the UCRI leader again placed his party in direct opposition to the popular concept of economic nationalism when he proposed to Congress a bill giving the chief executive power to grant to private companies—domestic or foreign—concessions for the development of power resources. This was quite a controversial issue, even within the President's own party. UCRP congressmen boycotted the sessions at which the bill was discussed while some Conservatives joined the boycott and others voted against the bill. In order to obtain passage in the Chamber of Deputies Frondizi needed the votes of 97 of the 111 UCRI members in that house. He had to resort to intimidation to obtain this majority. At first, many Intransigent Radicals joined the opposition boycott, but when the President threatened to have them removed from the party, most returned and voted for the bill.[9] The problems involved in getting the power concessions bill passed were typical of the troubles facing Frondizi in Congress after the UCRI majority in the lower house was severely reduced.

❋   ❋   ❋

In December, 1960, the UCRI National Convention wrote a new electoral platform. The ideals of the Declaration of Avellaneda, which Frondizi had ignored, were replaced by the far more conservative Declaration of Chascomús. While the former program had called for "nationalization of energy, transportation [and] fuel," the new one said "private, national or foreign enterprises that mobilize our proven natural resources ought not be hindered by useless bureaucratic caution." The 1960 National Convention also substituted such statements as "stimulation of agricultural production," "mechanization of agriculture," and "encouragement of farm cooperatives" for the 1958

---

[9] See the *Hispanic American Report*, XIII:9 (September, 1960), p. 641. The next month the UCRI National Committee removed three Intransigent Radical congressmen from the party and suspended six others for their failure to vote for this bill.

promise of "profound and immediate agrarian reform." The new platform was in essence a ratification of the policies followed by the Frondizi administration for two and a half years. Although the new platform was accepted by a vast majority of the Intransigent Radicals, showing the degree of control wielded by Frondizi, a few UCRI members left the party at this time. These men refused to move to the right with the rest of the party; they claimed to represent the true ideals of Intransigent Radicalism, that is, the program of 1958.

At the same time that the UCRI was moving to the right the Popular Radicals appear to have moved to the left. Originally the UCRP had been considered the more moderate wing of the old UCR; however, by 1961 the positions of the two Radical parties were virtually reversed. By this time the UCRP was claiming to be *the* nationalist party. On the other hand the Popular Radicals continued to be handicapped by the lack of leadership of the type exerted by Frondizi in the UCRI. Even after receiving the UCRP presidential nomination in 1958 Balbín was not recognized as the party leader by all its members. Also the continued existence of the MIN, MIR and *Núcleo Unidad* within the UCRP was not beneficial to the party. As was the case with its principle rival, the UCRP lost a small part of its membership late in 1960 when some Popular Radicals left to form the *Unión Cívica*. This new group, which was evidently composed of the former left wing of the party, immediately demanded the removal of Frondizi's conservative Minister of Economics, Alvaro Alsogaray, and of Toranzo Montero, the anti-Perón Commander-in-Chief of the Army, and legalization of Peronist parties.[10]

❀   ❀   ❀

Throughout his term Frondizi's relations with leaders of the armed forces were strained, at best. Most of the ranking members of the military had favored Ricardo Balbín and the UCRP in the 1958 elections. The military was opposed to the program Frondizi had long espoused, and this opposition was accentuated by his appeal for Peronist support in 1958 and by his acceptance of Communist aid in the election of that year. There were some generals who wanted to keep Frondizi from being inaugurated, but they were in a minority in 1958.

Throughout his first three years in office Frondizi was faced with

---

[10] All of these were soon realized.

a wave of strikes, riots, and attempted coups—some led by the Peronists and Communists, others by sectors of the military.[11] He was able to quell this violence only through the use of the armed forces. In order to retain the support of the military the President was forced to give its leaders an increasingly large voice in policy making. During this period, there was a virtually constant power struggle going on within the upper echelons of the Army and Navy; Frondizi had to shuffle constantly the membership of the military ministries in an attempt to appease whatever group was temporarily in control of the armed services. In September, 1961, the leaders of the Army forced the dismissal of the Foreign Minister who had aroused their wrath by arranging a meeting between Frondizi and Ernesto Guevara. Just five months later they demanded, and obtained, the removal of the successor to this position. He had abstained on the vote to censure Cuba at the 1962 Punta del Este meeting. It was also pressure from the military leaders that led to the appointment of Alsogaray as Minister of Economics and to the break in diplomatic relations with Cuba in February, 1962.[12] There are some who would claim that by 1962 Frondizi was a mere puppet of the military. While this would seem to be somewhat of an exaggeration, the military leaders had by this time obtained a virtual veto power over executive action.

At least part of the military's distaste for Frondizi was a result of the President's policy toward the Peronists, usually referred to "integrationism." Ever since 1957 Frondizi and Frigerio had been trying to integrate the mass of the Peronist movement into Intransigent Radicalism. Much of the middle class of the interior provinces and new industrialist upper class of Buenos Aires and Rosario, which had been largely Peronist between 1945 and 1957, was won over to the UCRI by 1958. However, it was the support of the urban working class—which, by and large, cast blank ballots in 1957 and 1960 and voted for the UCRI in 1958 on orders from Perón—that Frondizi and the UCRI needed in order to be assured of continued electoral success.

As the general elections of 1961-1962[13] approached, Frondizi and

---

[11] The *New York Times* [March 25, 1960, p. 10] reported that "since last July twenty-one persons have died as a result of terrorism and sabotage. More than 300 bombs have exploded."

[12] Lee Luna, *op. cit.*, pp. 46, 91.

[13] Although the general elections were scheduled for March 17, 1962, six of

the UCRI stepped up their campaign for Peronist support. The publications of the UCRI became more pro-Peronist than ever before. One spoke with pride of Peronist support of Intransigent Radicalism in 1958, and in comparing two movements said, "they have identical national views."[14] For a while it appeared that Frondizi was going to continue to prohibit the nomination of Peronist candidates, blame this on the armed forces, and hope that the UCRI could obtain enough Peronist votes to defeat its archenemy, the UCRP. However, shortly before the March elections the President announced that Peronists might freely campaign for any or all public offices (they were forced to do so under the labels of the many neo-Peronist parties since the Peronist Party, as such, was still illegal). There are about as many reasons put forth for the decision to allow Peronist candidates as there are commentators. Frondizi, himself, has said, "I have always been a decided partisan of equality of rights for all Argentines; in my presidential campaign I sustained the principle of equality without exclusions."[15] He went on to claim that he had prohibited Peronist candidates in 1960 because at that time the movement was actively engaged in illegal activities which had ceased by 1962.[16] The author is inclined to believe that Frondizi simply overestimated the success of his integration policy. This overconfidence may also have been accentuated by UCRI victories in the pilot elections held in December, 1961, and January and February of 1962.

With Peronist candidates on the ballots the 1962 elections were a three way struggle—for the first time since their formation, the UCRI and UCRP had real electoral competition. It is quite difficult to determine the actual choice presented by these three groups. For example, the Peronists appear to have offered only vague promises of a return to "the good old days."

The UCRP program was in some ways a negative one. The party campaigned against the petroleum contracts granted American firms and against the agreement made by Frondizi with the International Monetary Fund. UCRP candidates labeled intervention in trade unions

---

the nation's twenty-two provinces held their elections early (between December and February).

[14] Comisión Nacional de Difusión del Plan de Desarrollo. *La UCRI, Palanca del Desarrollo Nacional y la Justicia Social* (Buenos Aires: Ediciones UCRI, 1961), pp. 28-33.

[15] Luna, *op. cit.*, p. 204.

[16] *Ibid.*, p. 205.

"a return to Peronism," and the power concessions "a sellout to foreign imperialism." Popular Radicals continued to pledge their support of the Declaration of Avellaneda, which the UCRI had abandoned in 1960, and insisted that they formed the liberal and nationalist segment of Argentine Radicalism.

Instead of defending the policies of the Frondizi administration, the UCRI continued to attempt to enlist the support of Peronism. Yet at the same time, party leaders were posing as the only alternative to a return to Peronism. In an attempt to polarize the electorate UCRI candidates pictured the elections as an either-or proposition: Peronism or Intransigent Radicalism. Voters were told that a vote for the UCRP, Christian Democrats or Conservatives was in actuality a vote for the Peronists and for the return of Perón.

The results of the congressional election were the following:

Party	Vote	Per Cent	Seats
Peronists	2,999,146	31.9	41
UCRI	2,301,397	24.5	38
UCRP	1,875,587	19.9	8
Other parties	1,951,575	20.9	9
Blank ballots	262,020	2.8	—
Totals	9,389,725	100.0	96

Both Peronists and Intransigent Radicals increased their percentage of the popular vote at the expense of the Popular Radicals and minor parties. Almost one-third of the electorate voted for Peronists who surpassed the UCRI by about 700,000 votes and the UCRP by 1,100,-000. Peronist gubernatorial candidates were victorious in nine of the country's twenty-two provinces, including all-important Buenos Aires, while the UCRI carried three provinces (they had won five in the early elections). Popular Radicals won only in Córdoba.

The UCRI lost its congressional majority for the first time since 1958. The new Chamber of Deputies would have been composed of 81 Intransigent Radicals, 60 Popular Radicals, 41 Peronists, and 10 members of minor parties.

❖   ❖   ❖

The results of the 1962 elections marked the beginning of the end for President Frondizi. The day after the elections the President yielded to military pressure and intervened in five of the provinces won by the Peronists. This action accomplished little or nothing. It was not enough to satisfy the leaders of the armed forces and too much as far as opposition parties were concerned; even powerful UCRI members were angered by the action. The Minister of Interior, Alfredo Vítolo, resigned rather than sign the intervention decrees, and the UCRI governor of Buenos Aires announced that he would have resisted forcefully intervention in his province had there been any chance of success.

For ten days after the elections Argentina was in a state of confusion. There were constant rumors of a military coup. Frondizi attempted to form a coalition government, but even the UCRP refused to agree to this. He then asked Pedro Aramburu to talk to the military and civilian leaders in an attempt to find a means of ending the crisis. Aramburu eventually decided that the only solution was Frondizi's resignation. On March twenty-fourth, Navy leaders demanded that the President resign. Five days later came the apparently inevitable coup. Frondizi was "arrested" by leaders of the Army, Navy, and Air Force, and flown to the island prison of Martín García. As the nation was without a vice-president, the President of the Senate, José María Guido, was sworn in as Provisional President. The second period of Radical rule ended in the same manner as the first.

Chapter VIII

The Provisional Government: 1962-1963

For the first several days after his inauguration José María Guido devoted much of his energies to obtaining recognition of the constitutionality of his administration by the judiciary, and to attempts to prolong legally his term of office. The first was accomplished rather simply; however, Congress was not at all anxious to amend the succession law in order to grant the second.

On April twenty-fourth Guido issued an executive decree annulling all provincial elections held since December 1, 1961, and at the same time intervened in all the provinces. The next day he went a step farther and annulled all congressional elections held during the past five months. In May another decree recessed Congress indefinitely (the lower house had been left without a quorum by the earlier decree annulling the 1962 elections). Three months later this decree was replaced with another which simply dissolved Congress.

Neither of the Radical parties was united in its reaction to the policies of the Guido administration. During the last nine months of 1962 the UCRI was divided into three definite factions led by Alfredo García (former Chairman of the party's National Committee), Alfredo Vítolo (Frondizi's Minister of Interior), and Oscar Alende (former Governor of Buenos Aires).

Although he was the titular head of the party until late in the year, García's prestige within the UCRI declined steadily between April and August. Under his chairmanship, the National Committee cooperated to a certain extent with the administration. This "soft line" came under increasing criticism by influential party members, and in June the National Convention formally repudiated the policies of García and his National Committee.

Vítolo's sector of the party, known as the *Movimiento Nacional y*

Combatiente (MNC), was quite vociferous in its condemnation of the provisional administration which it called "the illegal de facto regime." Vítolo was bitterly opposed to Frondizi's interventon in the provinces won by Peronists—in fact, he resigned from the cabinet rather than sign the intervention decrees—but he was even more opposed to the overthrow of the President. In general, the MNC espoused: the return to office of Frondizi, respect for the results of the 1962 elections, reopening of Congress, removal of interventors from the provinces, and complete legalization of Peronism.

In August, the Alende faction gained control of the national apparatus of the UCRI; by the end of the year it was probably the largest single faction within the party. Its leader broke with Frondizi in March due to the intervention decrees. During the first few weeks in April the *alendistas* seemed inclined to support the new President; however, this faction also passed into the opposition before long, and by the end of the year its members were condemning the government as vigorously as the MNC. Although opposed, in principle, to the voiding of the March elections and the closing of Congress, the *alendistas* soon began to espouse new general elections for all positions from president and congressmen down to provincial and municipal officials. The position of Alende, himself, during the last few months of 1962 was one of vacillation. At one moment he said that Frondizi was still the President of Argentina and should be returned to office; at the next, he appeared to be seeking the UCRI presidential nomination. In November some of his supporters began rumors that Frondizi had given his blessings to Alende's candidacy; this was vigorously denied by members of other UCRI factions who also had visited the imprisoned former President.

There was also some internal dissension within the UCRP, but it did not take the same form it did within the UCRI. The Popular Radicals had always been split into definite intraparty organizations, and disputes in 1962 generally followed the lines of these factions.

The largest group, under the leadership of Ricardo Balbín, was incensed at Frondizi's intervention decree of March nineteenth, and many members were not particularly unhappy with his overthrow. (In fact the party's refusal to serve in a coalition cabinet may well have removed the President's last chance to remain in office.) At first it appeared that the UCRP would support the new administration. Its National Convention, however, conditioned support upon Guido's will-

ingness to respect the results of the March elections—which had severely reduced UCRP representation in Congress—and to allow the
victorious Peronists to take office. Thus, when the President voided
the elections and recessed Congress the UCRP officially moved into
the opposition.

Not all Popular Radicals were willing to follow the leadership of
Balbín; some of them—primarily from the *Núcleo Unidad* sector—
were convinced that Peronists must never be allowed to hold public
office. These Unionists held several cabinet posts between April and
September (the period in which the most extreme anti-Peronist sector of the armed forces was in control).

By November the UCRP National Committee gave up its demands
that those elected in March be allowed to take office. The official
position of the party was changed to favor new elections "held as soon
as possible and open to all democratic national parties."

❀   ❀   ❀

Probably the most important action[1] of the provisional government,
as far as the Radical Parties were concerned, was the promulgation in
July, 1962, of a new Statute of Political Parties and Law of Elections
(in actuality, both were decrees, Congress having long since been dissolved). According to the provisions of the former, existing parties
retained legal recognition only in those provinces wherein they had
received at least 3 per cent of the total vote in the last valid elections.
This section of the decree accomplished two of the major aims of the
government: limiting the steadily increasing number of political parties, and proscribing the major Peronist parties. The 3 per cent requirement did reduce the number of legally recognized parties from
sixty-three to twenty-three, and by stating that this requirement must
have been met in the last *valid* elections (thus excluding those of
March, 1962, which were annulled) most of the Peronist parties were
denied juridic personality. Parties wishing to act in provinces in
which they had not met the above requirements were forced to apply
to special electoral courts for recognition. In order to obtain this
recognition the party had to obtain the membership of a relatively
large number of qualified voters in the province in question and to
gain official approval of its Declaration of Principles, Program of

---

[1] Other than the decision to hold elections and return to constitutional government.

Action and Party Constitution. There were several additional restrictions aimed at the Peronists.[2] The Statute of Political Parties also distinguished between national and provincial parties. The first were those organized in a single district, while the second were those which might legally operate in more than half of the provinces. Only national parties were to be allowed to nominate candidates for president and vice-president. At the time of the promulgation of the decree this would have meant no more than four candidates: those of the UCRI, UCRP, Christian Democrats, and Conservatives.

The Law of Elections substituted the d'Hondt system of proportional representation for the incomplete list established in 1912 by the long-revered Sáenz Peña Law. According to this decree, proportional representation was to be used in the selection of senators from the capital, and all the national deputies and presidential electors. There was no mention at this time of the procedure to be followed in the election of provincial or municipal officials.

In November both the Statute of Political Parties and Law of Elections were amended—again by decree. Changes in the former included: dropping the provision that only "national parties" could nominate presidential candidates, altering slightly the number of names required on petitions for recognition, and waiving this requirement altogether for parties which in the last valid elections had received 3 per cent of the vote in at least three provinces. While the original Law of Elections had required the use of proportional representation only in the election of national officials, a new decree extended its use to all elections. This was in direct conflict with several provincial constitutions which called for the use of an incomplete list or single member districts. The requirement that governors and mayors be elected by proportional representation necessitated even greater changes in local constitutions. Since a single office cannot be divided among several parties, it was necessary to establish electoral colleges for these positions; electors could then be chosen by means of the d'Hondt system.

As finally amended the Statute of Political Parties did not appear to effect adversely either the UCRI or UCRP. It was generally as-

---

[2] Prospective parties had to promise not to rely upon persons or ideas outside the nation, nor to advocate the return of the Peronist regime, nor use any of its songs, slogans or symbols. Furthermore, party names could not be derived from those of individuals.

sumed, however, that the Law of Elections would be greatly to the detriment of at least one of the Radical parties. No longer would two or three parties be able to obtain virtually all elective offices.

*　*　*

Throughout the 1963 election campaign the activities of the UCRI and UCRP differed greatly. Intransigent Radicals devoted much of their energies to the attempt to form a large electoral coalition, while Popular Radicals early let it be known that they were going to the polls alone. Another important difference, which was somewhat surprising in view of the past histories of the parties, was the fact that factionalism hurt the UCRI greatly, while the UCRP was probably as unified as at any time in its six-year existence.

Beginning in late 1962 the Peronists, Intransigent Radicals and members of several smaller parties (including the Christian Democrats, Federal Union, Federal Party, and National Front Movement) attempted to put together a coalition known as the National and Popular Front (FNP). The Christian Democrats soon withdrew from these negotiations claiming that the economic program which the UCRI was intent upon imposing upon the FNP was far too conservative for such an alliance. There remained basically the same coalition that swept the 1958 elections: Peronists, Intransigent Radicals, and Social Christians.

For the next several months the leaders of these groups argued over joint candidates and the points to be included in an electoral platform. One of the major stumbling blocks to FNP unity was the choice of a presidential candidate. At first the Peronists and Intransigent Radicals each insisted that the nominee come from their ranks. Then in April an executive decree prohibited the nomination of candidates for executive office by the Peronists; they were to be allowed to enter candidates only for the Chamber of Deputies, provincial legislatures, and city councils. This still did not solve the problem, for the Peronists were unable to do anything until they received orders from their exiled leader in Madrid. Matters were further complicated when the partisans of Oscar Alende began to campaign as though Alende had already received the FNP nomination. Finally, as the deadline for filing approached, the UCRI National Convention was called to nominate party candidates. The nominations for president and vice-president were given to Alende and Silvestre Begnis—with the understanding that these men would step down if the National and Popular

Front should agree upon candidates.

In May the Peronists suddenly announced that they were going to support Vicente Solano Lima, the leader of the Popular Conservative Party, for the presidency and Silvestre Begnis for the vice-presidency. The word from Madrid had come. Both Frondizi and Frigerio immediately announced their support of Lima.

Begnis quickly resigned as the UCRI vice-presidential candidate in order to accept this position on the FNP ticket. Alende, however, refused to renounce his candidacy. While admitting that he had received the UCRI nomination upon the condition that there was no FNP candidate, he vehemently denounced the candidacy of Lima, saying that it was impossible for a Conservative to be the presidential nominee of the reform-minded National and Popular Front. He also pointed out that the FNP candidate should be agreed upon by all the Front's component parties, and not imposed by the exiled ex-dictator. All of this split the UCRI down the middle. Intransigent Radicals lined up behind Frondizi and Alende.

On June twentieth it was announced that the April decree which prohibited the nomination of candidates for executive office by Peronists was henceforth extended "to all those parties, regardless of their name, that present the same candidates for presidential and vice-presidential electors or gubernatorial electors that the Popular Union has attempted to make its own."[3] This then meant that Peronists could not even vote as a block for the executive candidates of another party. Word soon came from Perón that his followers should resort to the casting of blank votes as they had done in 1957 and 1960; Lima announced that his Popular Conservatives would also cast blank ballots. Refusing to switch his support to Alende, Frondizi asked UCRI members to vote in the same manner as the Peronists and Popular Conservatives.

While confusion reigned in the UCRI, the Popular Radicals were waging a quiet, but effective campaign. UCRP leaders early let it be known that they would have nothing to do with electoral alliances, and thus the party escaped the chaos in and among the FNP parties. Still, the UCRP was not without electoral problems. Its most logical candidate for the presidential nomination, Ricardo Balbín, announced that under no circumstances would he run for office. The ensuing intra-

---

[3] Decree #4874/63, Article I.

party struggle for the nomination was relatively brief and without the bitterness that took place in the UCRI. Long before the National Convention met it was well known that Arturo Illia would be the party nominee.

There were probably two primary reasons for the nomination of Illia: he was the only Popular Radical ever elected to executive office (he was elected Governor of Córdoba in the later annulled elections of 1962), and in spite of a long political career, he had few real enemies. A Radical since his high school days, Illia had served as a provincial legislator, vice-governor and congressman before his gubernatorial election in 1962. During the campaign Illia emphasized his opposition to the economic policies of the UCRI administration. He promised to annul the petroleum contracts granted foreign companies between 1958 and 1962, and suggested that foreign electricity concessions at least be renegotiated. He attacked the proscription of Peronist candidates and promised all political parties juridic equality. He also promised to annul the Frondizi decrees, which had limited the right to strike.

*　　*　　*

On July seventh more than nine million Argentines (about 82 per cent of the nation's qualified voters) went to the polls to choose 476 presidential and vice-presidential electors, 192 deputies, 1,128 gubernatorial electors, almost 1,000 provincial legislators and innumerable municipal officials. The elections were carried out in a peaceful and, it is generally agreed, honest manner.

Even from the early returns it was obvious that the Popular Radicals were going to roll up large pluralities in most areas. The final tabulations showed that the UCRP received over 25 per cent of the vote, outdistancing its nearest competitor, the UCRI, by almost 1,000,000 votes. However, due to the new electoral system, Popular Radicals received only 71 of the 192 seats in the Chamber of Deputies. Intransigent Radicals obtained 41, (quite a respectable number considering the fact that Frondizi had asked UCRI members to cast blank ballots), while the other 80 were divided among 23 different parties.

UCRP candidates were victorious in the gubernatorial races in thirteen of the twenty-two provinces; three Conservatives and two Intransigent Radicals also were elected. The other four governorships went to the candidates of minor parties. Popular Radicals gained a plurality of the seats in most of the provincial legislatures, but in only three of them did they receive an absolute majority.

Illia rolled up an impressive plurality in the presidential election, but fell far short of a majority of the electoral votes. The UCRP candidate received about 2,440,000 popular votes to 1,590,000 for Alende and 1,360,000 for Pedro Aramburu (the candidate of the Progressive Democrats and the newly formed Union of the Argentine People); no other candidate received as many as 500,000 votes. The tally of electoral votes showed Illia with 169 (70 less than the 239 needed for victory), 109 for Alende, and 74 for Aramburu; the other 124 were divided among a great many candidates, none of whom received as many as 30.

For several days after the election there were many meetings among the leaders of various parties in an effort to form the winning coalition in the electoral college. Several commentators predicted that these negotiations would lead to the reunification of the UCR, or at least most factions of it; the first stage of this was to be the support of Illia by UCRI electors. Such rumors were quickly dispelled when the UCRI National Convention decided that the party's electors should vote for Alende. When the electoral college met Illia was the overwhelming choice.

On October 12, 1963, Arturo Illia was inaugurated. After an interlude of only nineteen months, the Radicals returned to power.

Chapter IX

Radicalism Today

In 1958 the UCRI, united behind President Frondizi, was firmly in control of the governmental appartus of the republic; the UCRP, defeated decisively at the polls and divided into antagonistic ideological and personalistic factions, seemed incapable even of meaningful opposition. However, within six years the positions of two Radical parties were virtually reversed.

Ever since the election campaign of 1963 Intransigent Radicalism has been rent by intraparty conflict.[1] The struggle for control of the UCRI became readily apparent on June twentieth when Oscar Alende resigned as Chairman of the National Committee due to ideological differences with other committee members. The next day the committee was reorganized by *frondizistas* who chose Héctor Gómez Machado as Chairman. Soon after this, Alende withdrew his resignation and challenged the legality of Gómez' position. A federal judge first ruled in favor of Gómez and the *frondizistas*, but his decision was soon reversed.

It was not just within the National Committee that party differences were aired. On July twenty-sixth two separate UCRI National Conventions were held, with a majority of the delegates attending the meeting called by Alende. The major actions taken by this *partidista* convention included: (1) dissolution of the National Committee (a majority of whose members were *frentistas*) and its replacement by a National Executive Committee with Alende as its President; (2) establishment of a new *Mesa Directiva* for the convention (the former one was led

---

[1] The followers of Frondizi, who wanted to support the FNP at all costs are usually referred to as *frondizistas* or *frentistas*; Alende's supporters, who have placed the interests of the party above those of the Front, have been labeled *partidistas*, or *alendistas*.

[104]

by *frentista* leader); (3) telling all UCRI presidential electors to vote for Alende and Celestino Gelsi; and (4) expulsion from the party of three congressmen-elect—Arturo Zanichelli, Héctor Gómez Machado, and Pablo Fermín Oreja—for having conducted a blank ballot campaign prior to the July seventh elections. Some of the *alendista* delegates wanted to remove all *frondizistas* from the party; however, when it was pointed out that the National Convention had the power of expulsion only in the case of congressmen, nothing further was done in this respect.

At the same time, the *frentista* delegates, led by Julio Oyhanarte, held their own National Convention. Little was done by this group other than the deliverance of long speeches eulogizing Frondizi and condemning Alende. At the close of the convention it was announced that all *alendistas* had been expelled from the party[2] and that the Oyhanarte-led *Mesa Directiva* was assuming complete control over all UCRI affairs.

Each faction claimed that its National Convention was the legal spokesman for Intransigent Radicalism. The *alendista* claim was based upon the fact that a majority of the UCRI delegates attended its convention. On the other hand, the *frondizistas* pointed out that only the *Mesa Directiva* was empowered to set the time and place for National Convention meetings, and it was their convention which met when and where the Oyhanarte *Mesa* had ordered. The issue was resolved almost immediately when a National Electoral Court ruled in favor of the *alendistas*.

Beginning on August thirtieth, Alende's National Executive Committee intervened systematically in provincial party organizations which were hostile to his leadership. It began in La Pampa and Santa Fe where UCRI electors had not voted according to the orders of the *partidista* National Convention. By the middle of September, nine provincial organizations had been intervened; the others were already controlled by *alendistas*.

In September and October there was a great deal of talk about party unity; there were frequent rumors of a meeting to be held between Alende and either Frondizi or Oyhanarte. This meeting was never held, however, and in November the UCRI congressmen formed

---

[2] This announcement was made by Gómez Machado who at the same time was being expelled from the party by the *alendistas*.

two separate opposition groups as though there were two Intransigent Radical Parties.

Much of this confusion was resolved in April, 1964, when the *frondizistas* applied for legal recognition as a separate political party. At first they took the name Movement of Intransigent Radicalism (MIR); however, this label was vigorously opposed by the *alendistas* who claimed that it would lead to confusion with the Movement of Intransigence and Renovation [also MIR] sector of the UCRI. When this protest was upheld by the Electoral Court the name was changed to Movement of Integration and Development.[3]

Many factors—not the least of which is personalism—make it quite difficult to delineate clearly the ideological differences between these groups. In general, the UCRI is devoted to the principles of the Declaration of Avellaneda, while the MID advocates the Chascomús Program.[4] In other words, the latter proposes a continuation of the policies of the 1958-1962 Frondizi administration, while the former insists upon returning to the nationalistic program espoused by the left wing of radicalism between 1945 and 1958.

At this time there is no way accurately to measure the relative strength of the UCRI and MID: within the Chamber of Deputies the Intransigent Radicals split right down the middle with twenty members remaining in the old organization and nineteen joining the MID. Some indication of the electoral strength of these parties should be available after the March, 1965 congressional elections. While virtually any electoral result is possible, it would now appear that neither will do well in these elections; it may be expected that their total vote will fall short of that obtained in the past by Intransigent Radicals.

While the UCRI is in the process of disintegration, the Popular Radicals are evidently as well united as at any time in their short history. Even the nomination of a presidential candidate did not occasion the factional conflicts that some had forecast. What might have become quite a bitter struggle between the party's left and right wings was averted by the timely announcements by Balbín and Zavala that they would not be candidates for the nomination. The way was thus left open for the selection of a party moderate—Illia.

It is far too early to attempt any characterization of the UCRP ad-

---

[3] It should be remembered that two of the primary goals of the Frondizi administration were "integration" [of Peronism] and [industrial] "development."

[4] These two platforms are translated in Appendix B; see also *supra*, pp. 86, 90-91.

ministration, but one may assume that it will differ from the Frondizi government in at least one important aspect. The Popular Radicals are quite unlikely to continue the UCRI push for rapid industrialization at all costs. While this may come later, it now appears that the new President is intent upon at least a degree of economic stabilization as a first step. Already rather stringent import and export restrictions have been established.

The first act of President Illia to gain wide attention was his decree canceling all private petroleum concessions. This has been interpreted in the United States as illustrative of the anti-American, far left character of the new administration. Such a characterization is quite inaccurate, for as was pointed out before, the state oil company (YPF) is *the* symbol of economic nationalism in Argentina. It would be very unwise to use the cancellation of private oil concessions as the basis of predictions of the future course of action of Arturo Illia or his administration. The composition of his first cabinet would tend to dispel any notions that the President is about to embark upon a program of large-scale nationalization. At least six of the eight ministers were closely connected with the Aramburu administration (which was by no means leftist in nature), and the Ministry of Foreign Relations is headed by the leader of the most conservative Radical faction, Miguel A. Zavala Ortiz.

While it is unlikely that the UCRP administration will assume a definite leftist character, it is equally improbable that it will turn to extreme conservatism. In attempting to find a middle ground, Illia may well be criticized not for his policies, but for the relative lack of them.

Appendix A

Election Statistics

PRESIDENTIAL ELECTIONS: 1916-1963

	Votes	Per Cent	Electors
April 2, 1916			
Radical Civic Union	372,810	51.5	152
Conservative Party	154,549	21.3	104
Progressive Democrat Party	140,443	19.4	20
Socialist Party	56,107	7.8	14
Total	723,909	100.0	290
April 2, 1922			
Radical Civic Union	458,457	55.7	235
National Concentration	200,080	24.3	60
Progressive Democrat Party	73,222	8.9	10
Socialist Party	73,186	8.9	22
Principled UCR	18,435	2.2	6
Total	823,380	100.0	333
April 1, 1928			
Radical Civic Union	839,140	61.8	245
Antipersonalist UCR	439,178	32.4	71
Socialist Party	64,422	4.7	3
Progressive Democrat Party	14,173	1.1	0
Total	1,356,913	100.0	319
November 8, 1931			
Concordance	867,419	63.8	237
Democratic Socialist Alliance	488,535	36.2	122
Total	1,355,954	100.0	359
September 5, 1937			
Concordance	1,097,962	57.4	248
Radical Civic Union	815,190	42.6	128
Total	1,913,152	100.0	376
February 24, 1946			
Peronist Party	1,479,511	55.2	304
Radical Civic Union	1,210,822	44.8	72
Total	2,690,333	100.0	376
November 11, 1951			
Peronist Party	4,745,168	63.6	—
Radical Civic Union	2,415,750	32.5	—
Democratic Party	174,399	2.3	—
Communist Party	71,318	0.9	—
Socialist Party	54,920	0.7	—
Total	7,461,555	100.0	—

February 23, 1958

Intransigent UCR	4,070,875	44.9	319
Popular UCR	2,618,058	28.9	147
Christian Democrat Party	285,688	3.2	0
Socialist Party	264,746	2.9	0
Democratic Party	147,498	1.6	0
Progressive Democrat Party	125,432	1.4	0
Other parties	712,958	8.8	0
Blank ballots	838,243	9.3	—
Total	9,063,498	100.0	466

July 7, 1963

Popular UCR	2,440,536	26.2	169
Intransigent UCR	1,592,872	17.1	109
Union of the Argentine People	726,663	7.8	42
Progressive Democrat Party	632,701	6.8	32
Parties of the Center	499,822	5.4	29
Interior Parties	457,594	4.9	37
Christian Democrat Party	434,713	4.7	23
Argentine Socialist Party	282,799	3.1	12
Democratic Socialist Party	258,787	2.8	10
Other parties	304,792	3.3	13
Blank ballots	1,694,718	18.2	—
Total	9,325,997	100.0	476

COMPOSITION OF THE ARGENTINE CHAMBER OF DEPUTIES
1912 - 1930

Party	1912	1914	1916	1918	1920	1922	1924	1926	1928	1930
Radical Civic Union	11	28	44	56	84	91	72	60	92	98
Conservatives	14	25	28	19	14	14	14	15	14	12
Socialists	2	9	9	6	10	10	18	19	4	1
Liberal & Autonomist	3	7	3	3	3	3	5	5	5	2
Liberal	2	2	3	3	4	3	4	7	6	4
League of the South	1	3	2	—	—	—	—	—	—	—
National Union	7	5	—	—	—	—	—	—	—	—
Civic Union	5	6	—	—	—	—	—	—	—	—
Official Party	4	6	—	—	—	—	—	—	—	—
Constitutionalists	6	7	—	—	—	—	—	—	—	—
National Autonomists	1	1	—	—	—	—	—	—	—	—
Commerce & Industry	1	—	—	—	—	—	—	—	—	—
Provincial Union	—	2	4	4	3	3	3	2	2	1
Civic Concentration	—	1	1	1	1	—	—	1	1	—
Democratic Union	—	3	2	—	—	—	—	—	—	—
Popular Party	—	3	2	—	—	—	—	—	—	—
Democrats	—	1	1	—	—	—	—	—	—	—
Provincial Party	—	2	2	—	—	—	—	—	—	—
Independents	—	1	1	—	—	—	—	—	—	—
Coalition Party	—	1	—	—	—	—	—	—	—	—
Conservative Group	—	4	—	—	—	—	—	—	—	—
Progressive Democrats	—	—	8	14	19	14	14	9	—	3
Officialist Party	—	—	2	1	1	2	—	—	—	—
Popular Concentration	—	—	—	—	1	1	3	1	—	2
Situationalist Radicals	—	—	—	—	4	3	—	—	—	—
Blue Radicals	—	—	—	—	3	2	—	—	—	—
White Radicals	—	—	—	—	1	1	—	—	—	—
Black Radicals	—	—	—	—	1	—	—	—	—	—
Official Radicals	—	—	—	—	—	1	1	—	—	—
Intransigent Radicals	—	—	—	—	—	2	2	—	—	—
UCR Block	—	—	—	—	—	—	4	2	2	—
Lencinas UCR	—	—	—	—	—	—	—	2	1	1

	1912	1914	1916	1918	1920	1922	1924	1926	1928	1930
Antipersonalist UCR	—	—	—	—	—	—	3	7	5	3
Unified UCR	—	—	—	—	—	—	7	16	11	4
Commercial Union	—	—	—	—	—	—	1	—	—	—
National Democrats	—	—	—	—	—	—	2	—	—	—
Independ. Socialists	—	—	—	—	—	—	—	—	6	15
Single Front	—	—	—	—	—	—	—	—	1	1

1932 - 1954

	1932	1934	1936	1938	1940	1942	1946	1948	1951	1954
National Democrats	56	60	55	59	49	48	2	1	—	—
Socialists	43	43	25	5	5	17	—	—	—	—
Antipersonalist UCR	17	16	11	5	7	19	—	—	—	—
Unified UCR	4	4	4	5	5	2	—	—	—	—
Liberals	5	4	2	1	—	—	—	—	—	—
Independ. Socialists	11	6	2	—	—	—	—	—	—	—
Popular Party	2	2	2	—	—	—	—	—	—	—
Progressive Democrats	14	12	6	—	—	—	—	—	—	—
UCR Block	2	1	1	—	—	—	—	—	—	—
Provincial Defense	3	1	—	—	—	—	—	—	—	—
Radical Civic Union	—	2	40	64	76	63	44	45	14	14
Federalist UCR	—	1	1	—	—	—	—	—	—	—
Traditional UCR	—	1	1	—	—	2	—	—	—	—
Concurring UCR	—	—	4	5	4	—	—	—	—	—
Independents	—	—	2	—	—	—	2	—	—	—
Reorganized UCR	—	—	—	6	6	—	—	—	—	—
San Juan UCR	—	—	—	1	1	1	—	—	—	—
Tucumán UCR	—	—	—	—	—	1	—	—	—	—
Independent UCR	—	—	—	—	—	1	—	—	—	—
Santa Fe UCR	—	—	—	—	—	1	—	—	—	—
Agrarians	—	—	—	—	—	—	—	—	—	—
Laborites	—	—	—	—	—	—	2	—	—	—
Peronists	—	—	—	—	—	—	102	112	146	149

A COMPARISON OF POST-PERON ELECTIONS*
(in percentages)

	1957	1958	1960	1962	1963
Popular Radicals	23.2	25.4	23.7	19.9	25.4
Intransigent Radicals	21.2	41.8	20.6	24.5	16.2
Socialists	6.1	5.7	8.4	4.5	6.5
Conservatives	5.7	3.2	8.7	6.0	5.7
Christian Democrats	4.8	3.6	3.9	2.3	4.6
Progressive Democrats	3.3	1.8	2.7	1.7	5.8
Peronists & Neo-Peronists	2.4	2.7	2.4	31.9	7.0
Other parties	8.8	7.0	4.6	6.4	11.3
Blank ballots	24.5	8.8	24.9	2.8	17.5
Totals	100.0	100.0	100.0	100.0	100.0

*The 1957 figures are for the election of delegates to a Constitutional Convention; all others are for congressional elections.

Appendix B

Party Programs

INTRANSIGENT RADICAL CIVIC UNION
BASES OF POLITICAL ACTION

(Declaration of Avellaneda)

The following point out, at the present time, the great direction of political action of the Radical Civic Union.

Reestablishment of Federalism

Reestablishment of the federal and communal bases of Argentine constitutional organization in all institutional, educational, cultural and economic aspects. Provincialization of territories in order to incorporate their inhabitants into the federal representative regime.

Political Reform

A type of party organization which guarantees the direct intervention of citizens in the deliberations, decisions and control of the party. A system of primary elections. Political neutrality on the part of the administration. Political liberty for workers and employees.

Democratization of Culture

Educational reform which will stabilize the obligatory nature of secondary education, technical or agrarian, and guarantee to future generations equality of conditions and opportunities, and identical possibilities for the complete and free development of the physical, moral and cultural personality. Reestablishment of university reform. Reestablishment of liberty of conscience in the school.

Organization of Economic Democracy

Control of the economy on the basis of a plan fixed by organs which are representative of the popular will. Placement of natural resources, production and consumption, credit, industry, and international trade at the service of the people and not minority groups. Construction of a regime which subordinates the economy to the rights of man and mobilizes its resources not for the limited benefit of a few, but for national development and social welfare.

Nationalization of Public Services

Nationalization of energy, transportation, fuel and those capitalist concentrations that constitute cartels or monopolies, at the same time safeguarding the role of private initiative in its creative reality. Administration of the nationalized sectors by national, provincial, or communal entities or cooperatives, with the participation of technicians, users, producers and workers.

Industrial Democratization

Participation of technicians, employees and workers in the direction of industry. Freedom of unionization and the right to strike.

Agrarian Reform

Profound and immediate agrarian reform that brings the land—which ought not be mere merchandise—to the service of society. Organization of farm labor for the common use of machinery. Location of industries which use raw materials at the center of their production. Direct commercialization of farm products for their producers with state intervention to assure the value of production that should be obtained by producers.

Social Reform

The guarantee of: work conducted and remunerated with dignity, a decent standard of living, hygienic conditions, health protection, and access to culture; a social security system that includes the entire population from birth to death, subsidies for children, education, sickness, unemployment, marriage and maternity.

Financial Reform

Imposition of the largest financial loads on those with the great incomes. Reduction of bureaucratic costs. Defense of the purchasing power of money. Assurance of reasonable prices.

World-wide Economic Cooperation

Economic unity with neighboring countries and eventually with all of America. Creation of international organs to harmonize national economic planning.

The International Policy of Irigoyen

Defense of the economic, political and spiritual sovereignty of the country. Juridic equality of nations in world organization. No participation in political, economic or military blocks.

THE MOVEMENT OF INTEGRATION AND DEVELOPMENT PROGRAM OF POLITICAL ACTION

(Chascomús Platform)

The following points express, at this time, the objectives of political action of the MID; they affirm our concept that radicalism is the historic current of the emancipation of the Argentine people; their political roots are in our nationality and they constitute a requisitory against the materialist philosophies of the destiny of our nation.

Independent National Development

Since radicalism is the expression of the national conscience, its limits are those of the nation. The object of this stage of our history is expressed by the urgent necessity of national development. In order to overcome the dependent structure that asphyxiates our economy and impedes the elevation of the level of the cultural and material life of the people, it is necessary to create the real bases of a definitive national independence.

This historic mission applies to all the Argentine people without distinctions among ideology, party or social groups. The MID, complying with its historic mandate and due to the experience of February 23, 1958, has constituted itself as the instrument of national liberation; it fully retains its conviction that only the union of all Argentines—realizing active and militant action in the political-social area—can complete the task that political parties are not able to do alone. In order to obtain these objectives we proclaim the necessity to assure: legality for everyone without discrimination or proscription within the law, democracy, and the promoting of common action in order to promote national development.

National Unity

The great historical task of national development cannot be accomplished in a fragmented country whose components remain isolated and without communication. In the function of this national task federalism is the local expression of a single objective common to all the provinces. Federalism in this stage of development is the integration of geography that makes trade between different regions possible; the integration of the economy that impels the country to realize its interior energy, its industrial potential, and the mechanization of agriculture, thus definitely breaking the *porteño* colonial structure which was imposed upon the prostrate provincial economies; the integration of culture that foments and develops education, spiritual life, and the benefits of modern civilization in all areas of the Republic.

There cannot be incompatibility between the will of the nation and that of the provinces if federalism is to overcome its simple rhetorical formulation and be transformed into a true promotion of cultural and material progress of the interior of the Republic.

Bases of National Development

The independent economy of a country is the result of the harmonic development of agriculture, mining and industry based upon the exploitation of national resources.

The Argentine Republic has initiated a process of development and it will follow it to its conclusion, because there exists a clear and firm national conscience that desires it.

For this, the following are necessary:

1. A self-sufficiency of natural energy that can be obtained by the exploitation of petroleum, coal and all other sources of energy, and the erection all over the country of hydroelectric plants and petroleum refineries.
2. Intensification of the production of iron and steel; the exploitation of deposits of iron ore and coal and the construction of blast furnaces. Development of a petrochemical industry.
3. Construction of roads and new routes that will end the isolation of the productive regions.
   Reactivation, modernization and construction of airports and seaports. Promotion of aerial navigation and merchant marine.
   Remodeling of the railways and their coordination with highways; suppression of the deficits of the state railways through technical and administrative improvements.
4. Encouragement of mining through laws that will stimulate and protect investments.
5. Protection for national industries and for the exportation of its products. Protection against the competition of foreign monopolies.
6. Encouragement of the radication of capital and industry based upon the selection of geographic locations to promote the equal development over all the nation.
7. Stimulation of agricultural production. Incorporation of formerly unexploited areas into the productive process through a fiscal plan, and the protection of rural property and the granting of means of access to the producer. Intensification of the process of agrarian-transformation that will permit the rural producer to purchase land through credit. Protection of the agrarian family and mechanization of agriculture. Promotion of a higher level and a superior form of life for the rural population through electrification, education, and recreation. Encouragement of cooperatives.

For the most rapid attainment of these development objectives the state and the enterprises involved ought to coordinate their action within the guarantee of private initiative. All that serves the end of the independent development of our economy and that aids in its liberation from the international monopolies that have caused our subjection to the past ought to be promoted and stimulated. Private, national or foreign enterprises that mobilize our proven natural resources ought not be hindered by useless bureaucratic caution.

Social Policy

Workers and owners ought to harmonize their efforts in order to bring about the national objectives and to increase production. We defend the principles that assure to workers and owners an authentic representation.

[118]

There should be created a workers organization and an owners organization independent of political factors and of state interference. The working and owning sectors ought to coordinate, through the intermediate of their organizations, their activity in national development and in the entire process of national liberation. No sectional interest ought to be superior to the interest of the community in its march toward the creation of a superior form of national sovereignty. Only justice and social outlays adequate for each successive stage of economic development can effectively guarantee social well-being. Productivity should be increased by greater effort by the laborer and constant modernization of equipment and techniques of production. Salary policy ought to be based on the hierarchy or workers, employees and technicians according to their best professional capacity. The systems of social security ought to be integrated. There should be protection for women that work and for mothers.

Cultural Policy

Simultaneous action of the state and all the citizens in the expansion of teaching and in all the forms of culture. Liberty of teaching ought to be solidified in the training of technicians, men of science, investigators, highly qualified professionals, and specialized workers that the development of the country requires. Teaching ought to be identified with the objectives of the nation, and all its groups ought to concur in the spiritual, scientific, and technical formation of Argentines.

Educational structures ought to be revised, as should be their methods and goals so as to modernize them and adapt them to the national interest.

Culture should be stimulated. There should be a fusion of contemporary expressions with the traditionally rich Argentine inheritance so that culture can be nourished in the profound roots of nationality and flower in scientific, artistic, and spiritual manifestations that have their own features. Writers, artists, and students ought to be endowed with all classes of facilities to develop their creative faculties and contribute to the formation of national culture.

International Policy

We ratify the traditional Argentine policy of peace in respect to the principle of sovereignty and the principle of nonintervention. The nation should take part in organizations that promote peace, law and the conviviality of all the peoples of the world. The international policy of our nation should be prolonged in its national objectives in order to obtain the cooperation of nations more highly developed and in order to assure the solidarity of the peoples of Latin America in the common proposition of development. There should be action in favor of free international commerce and against discriminating and restrictive practices. There should be trade with all the nations of the world. We affirm the nation's sovereignty in defense against all internal or external attempts to diminish or subvert it.

POPULAR RADICAL CIVIC UNION
1963 ELECTORAL PLATFORM

OBJECTIVES: The Popular Radical Civic Union will mobilize the material and spiritual resources—by means of economic planning and social democracy—in order to obtain the following goals:

1. To establish domestic tranquility and to reestablish public faith.
2. To reaffirm national sovereignty.
3. To reclaim the fundamental bases of our economy, which has been compromised by the present petroleum, electricity and monetary policies.
4. To arrive at a harmonious development of the country, assuring the constant increase in production, and combining vigorous industrial development with intensification of agricultural and mining activities.
5. To assure a better distribution of national income to promote effective social mobility which in turn will facilitate economic security for working and middle classes.
6. To promote agrarian reform by modifying the economic, technical, legal and social structure of the land, to increase productivity and facilitate the obtaining of land by peasants.
7. To construct a social security system which will protect the people in all contingencies.
8. To respect the federal basis of our national organization, and to emancipate the provinces from political and economic centralism.
9. To promote a foreign policy which will help in the construction of a free and democratic world without fear or ignorance.

Morality and Democracy

A policy of national pacification. Freedom of the citizen and preservation of democracy. Elimination of all forms of violence. Inalterable maintenance of respect for liberty of religion. Repeal of repressive legislation. An amnesty law. A moral basis for public and political life. Electoral freedom for all—no exclusions. Legislation prohibiting administrative immorality and the illegal enrichment of public officials. Creation of conditions of life which exhalt the liberty and dignity of man. Protection for the family.

Culture and Education

Free access to culture at all its levels. The spiritual emancipation of man. Defense of the postulates of university reform. A national law of education which includes: The abandonment of encyclopedic formalism for scientific and humanistic knowledge. The eradication of illiteracy and school dropouts. A rational organization of education which will facilitate the moral and civic culture. A school which educates for liberty and social solidarity. Emphasis on regional education and the creation of rural schools. The diffusion of technical instruction in accordance with the needs of industrial development. The free functioning of pedagogical unions. An educational budget which is completely adequate for the task. The ultilization of modern audio-visual methods. Stimulation of the production and diffusion of Argentine books. Cultural interchange with all nations, especially those of the Americas. University extension service; aid to local libraries. Protection of the intellectual worker; steps to halt the emigration of scientific and technical personnel.

Social Security and Welfare

Sanctioning of a Labor Code and a Social Security Code. Guarantee of the right to strike; freedom of labor organization. A labor policy which permits the unity of Argentine syndicalism. A policy of full employment. A mobile minimum salary. Creation of a council of Labor-Management Relations. Establishment of a minimum pension level. Modernization of laws dealing with maternity and accident benefits. Protection of the working woman. Aid to children and the aged.

Economy

Creation of an Economic and Social Council to aid in the realization of a democratically planned economy. Affirmation of private initiative and full aid to the cooperative system in all its aspects. The assurance of democratic competition; elimination of monopolies. Control of the national economy by Argentines, not by the International Monetary Fund.

Agricultural Policy

Access to the land for the real producer. Intensification and diversification of agricultural production. Diminution of the costs of production. Division of latifundias which impede the development of the economy; elimination of the inconveniences of minifundias. Installation of centers of agricultural mechanization. Defense of export prices. Stimulation of the construction of agricultural cooperatives. Regional location of industries which are based on agricultural products.

Industrial Policy

Solution of problems arising from primary materials, machinery, energy and bureaucracies. An increase in the internal market and integration of regional markets. A credit policy designed to aid especially the small- and medium-sized industries. Technical improvements.

Foreign Trade

Foreign trade must be in accord with the public interest; it will be oriented toward the necessities of our program of national development. Diversification of exports. Commercial relations with all nations. Increase in the exportation of manufactured goods. Establishment of a strict list of priorities of imports.

Public Services and Electrical Energy

Public services must be available at reasonable prices and be oriented toward the supreme national objectives. Immediate revision of the electrical energy policy. Direct exploitation by the state of fundamental public services. Exploitation of the sources of hydraulic energy by the national government and/or the provinces. Establishment of rail rates based on national and provincial necessities. Rational and progressive betterment of transportation. An increase in the size and modernization of the Merchant Marine.

[121]

Petroleum

Rational exploitation by the state of petroleum and atomic energy to comply with the requirements of national development and to conserve natural resources. Immediate revision of the petroleum policy; nullity of petroleum concessions. Exclusive exploitation by YPF of petroleum and atomic energy. Neither the national government nor the provinces may grant concessions. Extensive exploitation of our mineral riches.

Federalism and Local Government

Rehabilitation of the federal bases of our national organization. Emancipation of the provinces from political and economic centralism without destroying the unity of the country. Promotion of regional markets. Administrative decentralization. Complete municipal autonomy for the City of Buenos Aires; popular election of the mayor.

National Defense

Decrease in the military budget to a level which is in accord with the real needs of the country. Modernization of the structure of the armed forces. Strict subordination of the armed forces to the civilian government.

Foreign Policy

A foreign policy based on the principles of Hipólito Irigoyen. Recuperation of the international prestige of the Republic by means of a policy which affirms the traditional independence of Argentina in its relations with the world. No participation in the alternatives of the cold war which engenders grave international tensions. Ratification of the policy of nonintervention and self-determination. Aid to the people who struggle for liberation from oppression. Strict solidarity with the peoples of Latin America in their struggle for the elimination of misery and ignorance. Action in inter-American and world organizations in a manner which reflects the will of the Latin American nations to live in peace. Opposition to the use of nuclear weapons. Reduction of arms. Affirmation of national sovereignty over the Malvinas and the Antarctic territory.

Bibliography

PART I
BOOKS AND PAMPHLETS

ARGENTINE POLITICAL PARTIES

Campobassi, José S., et al. *Los partidos políticos*. Buenos Aires: Cooperadora de Derecho y Ciencias Sociales, 1963.

Ciria, Alberto. *Partidos y poder en la Argentina moderna*. Buenos Aires: Jorge Alvarez Editorial, 1964.

Grattarola, Lázaro B. *Partidos políticos*. Santa Fe, Argentina: 1952.

Linares Quintana, Segundo V. *Los partidos políticos*. Buenos Aires: Editorial Alfa, 1945.

Melo, Carlos. *Los partidos políticos argentinos*. Córdoba, Argentina: Universidad de Córdoba, 1943.

*Puiggrós, Rodolfo. *Historia crítica de los partidos políticos argentinos*. Buenos Aires: Argumentos, 1956.

Scilingo, Francisco. *Decadencia de los partidos en la Argentina*. Buenos Aires: Editorial Araujo, 1945.

THE RADICAL CIVIC UNION

Almandos, Luis Reyna. *La demogogia radical y la tirania*. Buenos Aires: El Ateneo, 1919.

Almenara, Salvador. *Radicalismo: doctrina y historia*. Buenos Aires: Lanús, 1935.

Bianco, José. *La doctrina radical*. Buenos Aires: L. J. Rosso, 1927.

Bosch, Mariano Gregorio. *Historia del Partido Radical, la UCR*. Buenos Aires: L. J. Rosso, 1931.

Caballero, Ricardo. *La reconstrucción de la UCR*. Buenos Aires, 1930.

Gallo, Vicente C. *Por la democracia y las instituciones: propaganda cívica 1891-1921*. Buenos Aires: L. J. Rosso, 1921.

Gondra, Manuel Augusto. *Declinación del radicalismo y política del futuro*. Buenos Aires: El Mirador, 1957.

─────────. *El radicalismo y la política*. Buenos Aires: La Facultad, 1937.

Guitiérrez, Díaz A. *Nuestro radicalismo*. Buenos Aires: L. J. Rosso, 1930.

Lagos, Lauro. *Doctrina y acción radical*. Buenos Aires, 1930.

*Landenberger, Jorge W., and Conte, Francisco M. *Unión Cívica: su origen, organización y tendencias*. Buenos Aires, 1890.

Luzuriaga, Raúl Guillermo. *Centinela de libertad, 1914-1940*. Buenos Aires: A. López, 1940.

Maino, Alejandro. *Una estructuración doctrinaria del radicalismo*. Buenos Aires, 1954.

Mazo, Gabriel del. *Breve historia del radicalismo*. Buenos Aires: Coepla, 1964.

*─────────. *El radicalismo: notas sobre su historia y doctrina*. Buenos Aires: Ediciones Gure, 1959, 2 vols.

*─────────. *El radicalismo: el movimiento de intransigencia y renovación*. Buenos Aires: Ediciones Gure, 1957.

Nudelman, Santiago I. *El radicalismo al servicio de la libertad*. Buenos Aires: Editorial Jus, 1947.

Oyhanarte, Raúl. *Radicalismo de siempre*. La Plata, Argentina: Club Radical de Hombres Libres, 1932.

Peralta, W. R. *Historia de la Unión Cívica Radical*. Buenos Aires: G. Pesce, 1917.

Rabufetti, Luis Ernesto. *El dogma radical*. Buenos Aires: L. J. Rosso, 1943.

─────────

* Those works preceded by an asterisk (*) are the best points of departure for further reading.

Rodríguez, C. J. *Un mundo nuevo nace, Argentina radical.* Buenos Aires: La Fragua, 1963.

Rojas, Ricardo. *El radicalismo de mañana.* Buenos Aires: L. J. Rosso, 1932.

Spangenburg Leguizaman, Enrique J. *Los responsibles, el ejército y la Unión Cívica Radical ante la democracia argentina.* Buenos Aires: El Ateneo, 1936.

Torgoni, A. Roberto. *El radicalismo de hoy.* Buenos Aires: L. J. Rosso, 1932.

POPULAR RADICAL CIVIC UNION (UCRP)

Conferencias Radicales. La Plata, Argentina: Junta Central de La Plata, 1961.

Declaraciones y resoluciones, 1957-1959. Buenos Aires: Comité Nacional de la UCRP, 1959.

Decreto de intervención a los partidos políticos. Buenos Aires, 1962.

Dos años de gobierno partidario. Buenos Aires: Comité Nacional de la UCRP, 1961.

Es indespensible lograr una coincidencia nacional. Buenos Aires: Comité de la Provincia de Buenos Aires, 1962.

*Gobierno partidario, 1961-1963. Buenos Aires: Comité Nacional de la UCRP, 1963.

La Unión Cívica Radical del Pueblo ante la crisis institucional. La Plata, Argentina: Comité de la Provincia de Buenos Aires, 1962.

Principios de acción comunal. Buenos Aires: Comité de la Provincia de Buenos Aires, 1961.

INTRANSIGENT RADICAL CIVIC UNION (UCRI)

A un año de gobierno. Buenos Aires: Artes Gráficos Condor, 1959.

La conspiración reacionaria. Buenos Aires: Artes Gráficos Condor, 1959.

*Profesión de fe doctrinaria, Bases de acción política. Buenos Aires: Artes Gráficos Condor, 1960.

Una nueva actitud. Buenos Aires: Artes Gráficos Condor, 1959.

MOVEMENT OF INTEGRATION AND DEVELOPMENT (MID)

"Carta Orgáncia Nacional del Movimiento de Integración y Desarrollo." (mimeograph, 1964).

*Pan, Techo, Cultura y Libertad para 22 milliones de argentinos: Programa del MID para los comicios de Marzo de 1965. Buenos Aires: Editorial Escorpio, 1965.

Para salir de la crisis es necesario saber lo que quiere hacer y el MID lo sabe. Buenos Aires: Editorial Escorpio, 1965.

"Programa de Acción Política." (mimeograph, 1964).

LEANDRO N. ALEM

Alem, Leandro N. *Autonomismo y centralismo.* Buenos Aires: Editorial Raigal, 1954.

————. *Obra parlamentaria.* La Plata, Argentina, 1949.

**Farías Alem, Roberto. *Alem y democracia argentina.* Buenos Aires: Kraft, 1957.

Fernández de Burzaco y Barrios, Hugo. *Los antepasados de Alem fueron Gallegos.* Buenos Aires, 1955.

Gandolfi Herrero, Arístides. *Leandro N. Alem.* Buenos Aires: Editorial Sudamérica, 1953.

González Arrigi, Bernardo. *La vida atornamenta de Leandro Alem.* Buenos Aires: Editorial Signo, 1957.

Guerrero, Victor. *Alem: historia de un caudillo.* Buenos Aires: Editorial Raigal, 1951.

Manacorda, Telmo. *Alem: un caudillo, una época.* Buenos Aires: Editorial Sudamérica, 1941.

Salvadores, Antonio. *Alem y su profecía del 80*. Buenos Aires: Editorial Raigal, 1950.

Siviori, José P. *Alem: tribuno del pueblo*. Buenos Aires: Editorial Alpe, 1956.

HIPOLITO IRIGOYEN

Acosta, Alfredo. *El Dr. Hipólito Irigoyen*. Buenos Aires: J. A. Pellerano, 1918.

Amizor, René. *Irigoyen, apostol de la democracia americana*. Buenos Aires: L. J. Rosso, 1939.

Anonymous. *Hipólito Irigoyen para la historia*. Buenos Aires: J. F. Judari, 1934.

Arrebalzaga, Luis de. *Puñado de verdades*. Buenos Aires: Editorial Nacional, 1921.

Caballero, Ricardo. *Irigoyen: aspectos ignorados de una vida*. Rosario, Argentina, 1957.

Etchepareborda, Roberto. *Hipólito Irigoyen y el conflicto bélico*. Buenos Aires: Museo de la Casa de Gobierno, 1960.

————. *Irigoyen y el Congreso*. Buenos Aires: Editorial Raigal, 1952.

*Gálvez, Manuel. *Vida de Hipólito Irigoyen*. Buenos Aires: G. Kraft, 1939.

Guinazú, Ricardo H. *Irigoyen y el radicalismo*. Rosario, Argentina: A. Longo, [n.d.].

Irigoyen, Hipólito. *Discursos, escritos y polémicos del Dr. Hipólito Irigoyen*. Buenos Aires: T. Palumbo, 1923.

————. *Mi vida y mi doctrina*. Buenos Aires: Editorial Raigal, 1957.

*————. *Pueblo y gobierno*. Buenos Aires: Editorial Raigal, 1953.

Landa, José. *Hipólito Irigoyen visto por uno de sus médicos, estudio caracterológico de su personalidad*. Buenos Aires, 1958.

Marín, Marcial. *Irigoyen*. Buenos Aires: J. A. Santos, 1919.

Mazo, Gabriel del. *El pensamiento escrito de Irigoyen*. Buenos Aires, 1945.

————. *Irigoyen vivo*. Buenos Aires: Editorial Raigal, 1952.

Moreno Quintana, Lucio M. *La diplomacia de Irigoyen*. La Plata, Argentina: Editorial Inca, 1928.

Moro, Atilio. *Irigoyen: proceso a su gobierno*. Buenos Aires, 1929.

Oyhanarte, Horacio B. *El hombre Hipólito Irigoyen*. Buenos Aires: Editorial Claridad, 1945.

Rodríguez, Carlos J. *Irigoyen: su revolución política y social*. Buenos Aires: La Facultad, 1943.

Rodríguez Irigoyen, Luis. *Hipólito Irigoyen*. Buenos Aires: 1934.

Sánchez Sorondo, Matías G. *Historia de seis años*. Buenos Aires: Agencia General de Librería, 1923.

Sánchez Viamonte, Carlos. *El último caudillo*. Buenos Aires: Editorial Devenir, 1956.

Sommi, Luis Víctor. *Hipólito Irigoyen, su época y su vida*. Buenos Aires: Editorial Monteagudo, 1947.

Tristán, Lucia. *Irigoyen y intransigencia radical*. Buenos Aires: Indoamérica, 1955.

Villafane, Benjamín. *Irigoyen, la última dictador*. Buenos Aires: Moro, Tello y Compañía, 1922.

MARCELO T. ALVEAR

Alvear, Marcelo T. *Acción Democrática*. Buenos Aires: Editorial Cultura, 1937.

————. *Actuación parlamentaria*. Buenos Aires: La Epoca, 1922.

————. *Argentinos: Acción Cívica*. Buenos Aires: M. Gleizer, 1940.

————. *Democracia*. Buenos Aires: M. Gleizer, 1936.

Aramburu, Ricardo H. *El Presidente Alvear*. Buenos Aires: Casa Editorial Francoiberoamericana, 1922.

BIBLIOGRAPHY

Barroetaveña, Francisco A. *El gobierno de Alvear.* Buenos Aires, 1923.
*Luna, Felix. *Alvear.* Buenos Aires: Libros Argentinos, 1958.

ARTURO FRONDIZI

Cruz Machado, Daniel. *Frondizi: una conducta, un pensamiento.* Buenos Aires: Soluciones, 1957.
Frondizi, Arturo. *Argentina y América Latina.* Buenos Aires, 1958.
————. *Definiciones radicales.* La Plata, Argentina: UCR, 1955.
————. *Estrategía y táctica del movimiento nacional.* Buenos Aires: Desarrollo, 1964.
————. *Industria argentina y desarrollo nacional.* Buenos Aires: Editorial Qué, 1957.
————. *El gobierno y el comunismo.* Buenos Aires: Servicio de Prensa de la Presidencia de la Nación, 1960.
————. *Inflación y petróleo.* Buenos Aires: Editorial Escorpio, 1965.
————. *La lucha antiimperialista.* Buenos Aires: Ediciones Debate, 1955.
————. *Ni odio ni miedo: reconstruir el pais.* Buenos Aires: Servicio Editorial y Periodístico Argentina, 1956.
————. *Paz y libertad para todos los argentinos.* Buenos Aires: Soluciones, 1957.
————. *Petróleo y nación.* Buenos Aires: Transición, 1963.
————. *Petróleo y política.* Buenos Aires: Editorial Raigal, 1954.
————. *Política Económica Nacional.* Buenos Aires: Ediciones Arayú, 1963.
————. *Política Exterior Argentina.* Buenos Aires: Transición, 1963.
————. *El tratado de Río de Janeiro.* Buenos Aires, 1950.
Greco, Rafael. *Frondizi no puede ser Presidente.* Buenos Aires: Ediciones F. B., 1956.
*Luna, Felix. *Diálogos con Frondizi.* Buenos Aires: Editorial Desarrollo, 1963.
Morales Loza, Nestor. *Frondizi y la verdad.* Buenos Aires: Urania, 1957.
Rey, Esteban. *Es Frondizi un nuevo Perón?* Buenos Aires: Editorial Lucha Obrera, 1957.
Rivera, Enrique. *Peronismo y frondizismo.* Buenos Aires: Editorial Patria Grande, 1958.
Uzal, Francisco Hipólito. *Frondizi y la oligarquía.* Buenos Aires: Compañía Argentina de Editores, 1963.

ROGELIO FRIGERIO

Frigerio, Rogelio. *Las condiciones de victoría.* Montevideo: A. Monteverde, 1963.
————. *Los cuatros años.* Buenos Aires: Editorial Concordia, 1962.
————. *El pais de nuevo en la encrucijada.* Buenos Aires, 1960.
————. *El pueblo en el proceso nacional.* Buenos Aires, 1961.
————. *Unidad nacional o lucha de facciones.* Buenos Aires, 1961.
Ortiz, S. H. *El libro rojo de Rogelio Frigerio.* Montevideo: Editorial Verax, 1962.
Rey, Esteban. *Frigerio y la traición de la burguesía industrial.* Buenos Aires: A. Peña Lillo, 1959.

MEMOIR

Barrau, José. *Labor parlamentaria 1938-1941.* Buenos Aires: Edición del Autor, 1942.
Cárcano, Ramón. *Mis primeros ochenta años.* Buenos Aires: Editorial Sudamérica, 1943.
Colomba, Ramón. *El Congreso que yo he visto: 1934-1943.* Buenos Aires, 1951.
Dickmann, Enrique. *Recuerdos de un militante socialista.* Buenos Aires, 1949.
Gallo, Vicente C. *Desde la tribuna.* Buenos Aires: M. Gleizer, 1938.

[127]

Goldstraj, Manuel. *Años y errores, un cuarto siglo de política argentina.* Buenos Aires: Sophos, 1957.
————. *El camino del exilio.* Buenos Aires: Librería Anaconda, 1935.
*Gómez, Alejandro. *Política de entrega.* Buenos Aires: A Peña Lillo, 1963.
Justo, Juan Bautista. *Discursos y escritos políticos.* Buenos Aires, 1933.
Lebensohn, Moisés. *Pensamiento y acción.* Buenos Aires, 1956.
Noel, Carlos M. *Principios y orientaciones.* Buenos Aires: M. Gleizer, 1939.
*Perina, Emilio. *Detrás de la crisis.* Buenos Aires: Editorial Periplo, 1960.
Repetto, Nicolás. *Mi paso por la política.* Buenos Aires: Santiago Ruedo, 1956.

"REVOLUTION"

Allende, Oscar F. *Problemas fundamentales de la revolución de 16 de setiembre [de 1955].* Buenos Aires: Ediciones Signo, 1956.
Alvarez, Juan. *La guerras civiles argentinas.* Buenos Aires: Editorial Coyoacán, 1961.
Balestra, Juan. *El noventa.* Buenos Aires: La Facultad, 1935.
Caballero, Ricardo. *Irigoyen: la conspiración civil y militar del 4 de febrero de 1905.* Buenos Aires: Editorial Raigal, 1951.
Carril, Bonifacio del. *Crónica interna de la revolución libertadora.* Buenos Aires: Lumen, 1957.
————. *Problemas de la revolución y la democracia.* Buenos Aires: Emecé, 1956.
Etcheapareborda, Roberto. *La crisis de 1930.* Buenos Aires, 1958.
Galíndez, Bartolomé. *Apuntes de tres revoluciones: 1930, 1943, 1955.* Buenos Aires: Castro Barrera, 1956.
Josephs, Ray. *Argentine Diary.* New York: Random House, 1944.
Matienzo, José Nicolás. *La revolución de 1890.* Buenos Aires, 1926.
————. *La revolución de 1930.* Buenos Aires: Librería Anaconda, 1930.
Mendía, José. *La revolución.* Buenos Aires: Imprenta de Mendía y Martínez, 1890, 2 vols.
Perón, Juan Domingo. *Fuerza es el derecho de las bestias.* Montevideo: Cicerón, 1958.
————. *Tres revoluciones militares.* Buenos Aires: Escorpión, 1963.
Quesada, Julio Argentino. *Origines de la revolución de 6 de setiembre de 1930.* Buenos Aires: Librería Anaconda, 1930.
Rodríguez Araya, Agustín. *Revolución inconclusa.* Buenos Aires: Editorial Proceso, 1963.
*Sarobe, José María. *Memorias sobre la revolución de 6 de setiembre de 1930.* Buenos Aires: Ediciones Gure, 1957.
Sommi, Luis V. *La revolución del 90.* Buenos Aires: Editorial Monteagudo, 1948.
Tres Revoluciones. Buenos Aires: Editor Emilio Perrot, 1959.
Vedía y Mitre, Mariano de. *La revolución del 90.* Buenos Aires, 1926.
Zorraquín Becú, Horacio. *et al. Cuatro revoluciones argentinas.* Buenos Aires: Club Nicolás Avellaneda, 1960.

MISCELLANEOUS

Alexander, Robert J. *The Peron Era.* New York: Columbia University Press, 1951.
Amadeo, Mario. *Ayer, Hoy, Mañana.* Buenos Aires: Ediciones Gure, 1956.
————. *La encrucijada argentina.* Madrid: Ediciones y Publicaciones Españoles, 1956.
Ayarragaray, Lucas. *Cuestiones y problemas argentinas contemporáneos.* Buenos Aires: Lajouanne, 1930.
Bianco, José. *Vida de las instituciones políticas.* Buenos Aires: A Sanourin y Hijo, 1919.

BIBLIOGRAPHY

*Blanksten, George I. *Peron's Argentina*. Chicago: University of Chicago Press, 1953.

Bucich Escobar, Ismael. *Historia de los Presidentes Argentinos*. Buenos Aires: Ediciones Anaconda, 1934.

Carril, Bonifacio del. *La crisis argentina*. Buenos Aires: Emecé, 1960.

————. *Qué nos pasa a los Argentinos?* Buenos Aires: Edición del Autor, 1963.

Cossio, Carlos. *La política como consciencia*. Buenos Aires: Abeledo Perrot, 1957.

Frondizi, Silvio. *La crisis política argentina*. Buenos Aires: Ediciones A. D. I., 1946.

*Germani, Gino. *Estructura social de la Argentina*. Buenos Aires: Editorial Raigal, 1955.

Ghioldi, Américo. *De la tirania a la democracia social*. Buenos Aires: Ediciones Gure, 1956.

Greenup, Ruth and Leonard. *Revolution Before Breakfast*. Chapel Hill: University of North Carolina Press, 1947.

*Guardo, Ricardo C. *Horas difíciles*. Buenos Aires: A. Peña Lillo, 1963.

Ingenieros, José. *Sociología argentina*. Buenos Aires: Losada, 1946.

*Kennedy, John J. *Catholicism, Nationalism and Democracy in Argentina*. Notre Dame, Indiana: University of Notre Dame Press, 1958.

Labourdette, Alberto Jorge. *Argentina: 1962*. Buenos Aires: Edición del Autor, 1962.

MacDonald, Austin F. *Government of the Argentine Republic*. New York: Thomas Y. Crowell, 1942.

Matienzo, José N. *El gobierno representativo federal en la república argentina*. Madrid: Editorial América, 1937.

Mazo, Gabriel del. *La reforma universitaria*. Buenos Aires, 1947.

*Merchensky, Marcos. *Las corrientes ideológicas en la historia argentina*. Buenos Aires: Concordia, 1961.

Methol Ferré, Alberto. *La izquierda nacional en la Argentina*. Buenos Aires: Editorial Coyoacán, 1960.

Montemayor, Mariano. *Claves para entender un gobierno*. Buenos Aires: El Sol, 1960.

Noel, Carlos M. *3 de enero de 1941*. Buenos Aires: Peuser, 1943.

Nudelman, Santiago. *Justicia social*. Buenos Aires, 1953.

————. *Problemas de independencia económica*. Buenos Aires, 1955.

Ortiz, Ricardo. *Historia económica de la Argentina: 1850-1930*. Buenos Aires: Editorial Raigal, 1955.

Oyhanarte, Julio. *Lebensohn*. La Plata, Argentina: Línea Combatiente, 1956.

Peña, David. *La materia religiosa en la política argentina*. Buenos Aires: Editorial Bases, 1960.

Prieto, Ramón. *El Pacto*. Buenos Aires: Editorial En Marcha, 1963.

Rabinovitz, Bernardo. *Sucedió en la Argentina: lo que no se dijo*. Buenos Aires: Ediciones Gure, 1956.

Ramos, Jorge Abelardo. *Historia política del ejército argentino*. Buenos Aires: A. Peña Lillio, 1958.

————. *El Partido Comunista en la política argentina*. Buenos Aires: Editorial Coyoacán, 1962.

Real, Juan José. *30 años de historia argentina*. Buenos Aires: Ediciones Actualidad, 1962.

Rennie, Ysabel F. *The Argentine Republic*. New York: The Macmillan Co., 1945.

*Romero, José Luis. *Las ideas políticas en la Argentina*. Mexico: Fondo de Cultura Económica, 1946.

Sábato, Arturo. *Historia de los contratos petroleros.* Buenos Aires, 1963.
Saravia, José Manuel. *Argentina 1959.* Buenos Aires: Ediciones del Atlántico, 1959.
Solari, Juan Antonio. *Examen y responsibilidades de la situación argentina.* Buenos Aires: Editorial Bases, 1959.
————. *Por la reforma electoral.* Buenos Aires: Editorial Bases, 1961.
Strasser, Carlos. *Las izquierdas en el proceso político argentino.* Buenos Aires: Editorial Palestra, 1959.
Suhr-Horeis, A. E. *La crisis argentina desde mayo de 1958.* Buenos Aires: Ediciones Gure, 1958.
Tarditi, José R. *La crisis argentina.* Buenos Aires: Editorial Bases, 1962.
Tiscornia, Eduardo. *Qué pasa con la Argentina?* Buenos Aires: Tres Américas, 1962.
Weil, Felix. *Argentine Riddle.* New York: John Day Co., 1944.
Whitaker, Arthur P. *Argentine Upheaval.* New York: Frederick A. Praeger, 1956.
Zalduendo, Eduardo. *Geografía electoral de la Argentina.* Buenos Aires: Ediciones Ancora, 1958.

ARTICLES

Abalos, José Benjamín. "Testimonio," *Revista de Historia,* III (1958), pp. 95-98.
Acosta, Guillermo. "El radicalismo y su programa," *Hechos e Ideas,* II:6 (December, 1935), pp. 160-163.
Alba, Victor. "The Argentine Election," *New Leader,* XL:32 (August 12, 1957), pp. 3-4.
Alexander, Robert J. "After Perón—Frondizi?" *New Leader,* XXXVIII:19 (May 9, 1955), pp. 19-20.
————. "Argentina in Transition," *New Leader,* XLI:41 (November 10, 1958), pp. 10-12.
————. "New Chance for Argentine Democracy," *New Leader,* XLI:16 (May 18, 1958), pp. 8-9.
Alvear, Marcelo T. "Acotaciones al decreto de intervención a Santa Fe," *Hechos e Ideas,* II:5 (November, 1935), pp. 46-48.
————. "Conceptos del Dr. Alvear sobre el momento," *Hechos e Ideas,* IV:16 (November, 1936), pp. 405-409.
————. "Discurso de Dr. Alvear pronunciado en La Plata el 31 de octubre de 1935," *Hechos e Ideas,* II:6 (December, 1935), pp. 176-180.
————. "Discurso del Presidente del Comité Nacional de la UCR," *Hechos e Ideas,* IX:36 (March-April, 1940), pp. 353-357.
————. "Dos discursos de Dr. Alvear," *Hechos e Ideas,* VII:27 (March-April, 1938), pp. 201-208.
————. "Parrafos de un reciente discurso del Dr. Alvear," *Hechos e Ideas,* VI:22 (June, 1937), p. 10.
————. "Reflexiones sobra la libertad y la democracia," *Hechos e Ideas,* (January-February, 1938), pp. 80-87.
————. "Responsibilidades de la hora," *Hechos e Ideas,* I:1 (June, 1935), pp. 10-11.
Amado, Isaías R. "Contribución para la redacción de un programa del partido," *Revista Argentina de Ciencias Políticas,* XII:68 (May, 1916), pp. 91-110.
Bagú, Sergio. "Argentina 1961," *Cuadernos Americanos,* XX:6 (November-December, 1961), pp. 18-32.
————. "Argentina: una realidad revolucionaria," *Cuadernos Americanos,* XXVII:3 (May-June, 1946), pp. 7-41.

BIBLIOGRAPHY

Beals, Carleton. "Argentina vs. United States," *Current History*, L:5 (July, 1939), pp. 28-31.

Becerra, Olegario. "Interpretación radical de la revolución del 90," *Revista de Historia*, I (1957), pp. 52-55.

————. "La juventud radical y su congreso," *Hechos e Ideas*, VII:26 (January-February, 1938), pp. 67-70.

Carulla, Juan E. "Entretelones de la revolución de 1930," *Revista de Historia*, III (1958), pp. 119-122.

Cisneros, Carlos E. "La obra que la UCR debe realizar en el parlamento," *Hechos e Ideas*, III:9 (March, 1936), pp. 26-28.

"Convención Nacional de la Unión Cívica Radical," *Hechos e Ideas*, VI:22 (June, 1937), pp. 85-112.

Corvalán, Ernesto. "Pensamiento e ideas radicales," *Revista Argentina de Ciencias Políticas*, X:58 (July, 1915), pp. 411-413.

Cuneo, Dardo. "Las dos corrientes del movimiento obrero en el 90," *Revista de Historia*, I (1957), pp. 61-72.

"Declaraciones del Comité Nacional de la UCR," *Hechos e Ideas*, VI:25 (December, 1937), pp. 386-389.

Etchepareborda, Roberto. "Acción opositora durante la presidencia de Carlos Pelligrini (1890-1892)," *Boletín del Instituto de Historia Argentina*, III:7 (1961), pp. 1-51.

————. "Aspectos políticos de la crisis de 1930," *Revista de Historia*, III (1958), pp. 7-40.

————. "Cronología nacional [1928-1932]," *Revista de Historia*, III (1958), pp. 144-155.

————. "Entretelones del noventa," *Historia*, V:17 (July-September, 1959), pp. 106-118.

Fisk, Ysabel. "Argentina: The Thirteen Year Crisis," *Foreign Affairs*, XXII:2 (January, 1942), pp. 256-266.

Florit, Carlos Alberto. "El personalismo político argentino," *Estudios*, 530 (December, 1961), pp. 769-776.

Frondizi, Arturo. "Anti-Peronist Program: Freedom Comes First," *Nation*, CLXXXI:11 (September 17, 1955), pp. 238-239.

————. "Ha sonado para la América la hora de la ley, del derecho y de la colaboración entre las naciones que la integran," *La Justica*, XXVIII:343 (November, 1958), pp. 15-25.

Gallo, Vicente C. "Aspectos y enseñanzas de una obra," *Revista Argentina de Ciencias Políticas*, X:58 (July, 1915), pp. 329-336.

Giusti, Roberto F. "La sublevación civil y militar de 1930," *Revista de Historia*, III (1958), pp. 132-138.

Gómez, Rosendo A. "Intervention in Argentina 1860-1930," *Inter-American Economic Affairs*, I:3 (December, 1947), pp. 53-73.

Haring, Clarence. "Depression and Recovery in Argentina," *Foreign Affairs*, XIV:3 (April, 1936), pp. 506-519.

Hasbrouck, Alfred. "The Argentine Revolution of 1930," *Hispanic American Historical Review*, XVIII:3 (April, 1938), pp. 285-321.

Horowitz, Irving L. "Storm over Argentina," *The Nation*, CXCIV:13 (March 31, 1962), pp. 281-284.

Ilsley, Lucretia L. "The Argentine Constitutional Revision of 1949," *Journal of Politics*, XIV:2 (May, 1952), pp. 224-240.

Kennedy, John J. "Accountable Government in Argentina," *Foreign Affairs*, XXXVII:3 (April, 1959), pp. 453-462.

"La elección del General Perón—cifras de los escrutinios y nomina de los electos," *Hechos e Ideas*, XXII:92 (November, 1951), pp. 195-204.

Luna, Pelagio. "El radicalismo en las provincias," *Revista Argentina de Ciencias Políticas*, X:58 (July, 1915), pp. 386-394.

"Manifesto del Comité Nacional al pueblo de la República," *Hechos e Ideas*, II:5 (November, 1935), pp. 70-72.

M. A. R. "La elección presidencial y algunas de sus consecuencias," *Revista Argentina de Ciencias Políticas*, XII:70 (July, 1916), pp. 410-413.

"Marzo: mes electoral," *Revista Argentina de Ciencias Políticas*, IV:19 (April, 1912), pp. 76-78.

Matthews, Herbert L. "Argentina Moving Toward Democracy," *Foreign Policy Bulletin*, XXXVIII:10 (February 1, 1959), pp. 72-79.

Maupas, Leopoldo. "Trascendencias políticas de la nueva ley electoral," *Revista Argentina de Ciencias Políticas*, IV:22 (June, 1912), pp. 409-428.

Montes, Carlos. "Frondizi y los comunistas," *Estudios sobre Comunismo*, V:17 (July-September, 1957), pp. 118-124.

Murkland, Harry B. "Argentine Battleground," *Current History*, IX:50 (October, 1945), pp. 299-304.

Onis, Juan de. "Argentina Tested by Economic Realities," *Foreign Policy Bulletin*, CXLXI:21 (July 15, 1959), pp. 161-162.

Orona, Juan V. "Una logia poco conocida y la revolución del 6 de septiembre," *Revista de Historia*, III (1958), pp. 73-94.

Ortiz, Ricardo M. "El aspecto económico-social de la crisis de 1930," *Revista de Historia*, III (1958), pp. 41-72.

Palacios, Alfredo L. "Juicios del Senador Socialista Dr. Alfredo L. Palacios sobre la personalidad de Dr. Alvear," *Hechos e Ideas*, VI:22 (June, 1937), pp. 34-37.

Pérez Aznar, Ataulfo. "Esquema de las fuerzas políticas actuantes hasta 1890," *Revista de Historia*, I (1957), pp. 36-51.

Perkins, Jorge W. "Qué ha hecho crisis en la Argentina," *Nosotros*, 262 (March, 1931), pp. 225-239.

Piñedo, Federico. "Testimonio," *Revista de Historia*, III (1958), pp. 112-119.

"Plataforma electoral de la UCR de Córdoba," *Hechos e Ideas*, IX:35 (January-February, 1940), pp. 244-247.

"Plataformas electorales que sostendrá la UCR de la Capital sancionada por la H. Convención Nacional en los meses de diciembre de 1935 y enero de 1936," *Hechos e Ideas*, II:8 (February, 1936), pp. 376-379.

Potash, Robert A. "Argentina's Quest for Stability," *Current History*, XLII:246 (February, 1962), pp. 71-76.

————. "Argentine Political Parties: 1957-1958," *Journal of Inter-American Affairs*, I:4 (October, 1959), pp. 515-524.

Pozuelo, Claudio R. "El radicalismo argentino," *Revista Argentina de Ciencias Políticas*, X:58 (July, 1915), pp. 377-385.

Prack, Enrique B. "La misión del radicalismo," *Revista Argentina de Ciencias Políticas*, X:58 (July, 1915), pp. 405-406.

"Radicalismo y peronismo se identifican en su proyectos históricos," *Hechos e Ideas*, XII:47 (February, 1948), pp. 371-378.

Ratto, Francisco. "Testimonio," *Revista de Historia*, III (1958), pp. 109-111.

"Resolución del Comité Nacional de la Unión Cívica Radical frente al fraude Santafecino," *Hechos e Ideas*, V:19 (March, 1937), pp. 121-123.

"Resoluciones y sanciones de la H. Convención Nacional." *Hechos e Ideas*, VI:22 (June, 1937), pp. 113-141.

Rivarola, Victor E. "El partido radical y la juventud," *Revista Argentina de Ciencias Políticas*, X:58 (July, 1915), pp. 407-410.

Rodríguez Villar, Pacífico. "Las provincias argentinas y la Unión Cívica Radical *Hechos e Ideas*, I:1 (June, 1935), pp. 19-24.

R. R. "Resultados de la elección de marzo," *Revista Argentina de Ciencias Políticas*, VI:32 (May, 1913), pp. 199-203.

Sabattini, Amadeo. "Discurso-programa del Dr. Sabattini," *Hechos e Ideas*, II:ʊ (November, 1935), pp. 66-69.

————. "La obra del gobierno radical de Córdoba," *Hechos e Ideas*, V:21 (May, 1937), pp. 405-444.

Sagarna, Antonio. "Concepto del radicalismo argentino," *Revista Argentina de Ciencias Políticas*, X:58 (July, 1915), pp. 348-366.

Sagastume, Enrique A. "A Unión Cívica Radical en la provincia de Buenos Aires," *Revista Argentina de Ciencias Políticas*, X:58 (July, 1915), pp. 395-404.

Sánchez Sorondo, Matías. "6 septiembre de 1930," *Revista de Historia*, III (1958), pp. 98-109.

Santillán, Diego A. "El movimiento obrero argentino ante al golpe de estado del 6 de septiembre de 1930," *Revista de Historia*, III (1958), pp. 123-132.

Scotti, Elvio José. "Un año de gobierno constitucional," *Estudios*, XLVIII:504 (June, 1959), pp. 282-288.

Silvert, K. H. "The Annual Political Cycle in Argentina," *American Universities Field Staff Reports*, VIII:6 (December 12, 1961), pp. 1-12.

————. "Economics, Democracy, and Honesty: An Assessment of the Frondizi Regime," *American Universities Field Staff Reports*, VII:1 (April 10, 1960).

Snow, Peter G. "Argentine Radicalism: 1957-1963," *Journal of Inter-American Studies*, V:4 (October, 1963), pp. 507-531.

————. "Parties and Politics in Argentina," *Midwest Journal of Political Science*, IX:1 (February, 1965), pp. 1-36.

————. "The Evolution of the Argentine Electoral System," *Parliamentary Affairs*, XVIII:3 (Summer, 1965), pp. 330-336.

Solari, J. A. "La nueva situación argentina," *Cuadernos*, XXXI (July-August, 1958), pp. 73-76.

Sommi, Luis V. "La estructura económica-social de la Argentina en 1890," *Revista de Historia*, I (1957), pp. 18-35.

S. A. "New Hope for Argentina's Economy?" *World Today*, XV:10 (October, 1959), pp. 379-386.

"The Election Count," *Review of the River Plate*, LXXXIII:2391 (October 8, 1937), p. 3.

Villaroel, Raúl. "Breve estudio del partido radical santafecino," *Revista Argentina de Ciencias Políticas*, VII:41 (February, 1914), pp. 600-603.

Whitaker, Arthur P. "Social and Economic Crisis in Argentina," *Current History*, XL:236 (April, 1961), pp. 208-213, 218.

Wilmart, R. "El partido radical, su ubificación," *Revista Argentina de Ciencias Políticas*, X:58 (July, 1915), pp. 367-376.

Wilmart, W. "La elecciones de marzo-abril en la capital," *Revista Argentina de Ciencias Políticas*, VI:32 (May, 1913), pp. 117-132.

PART III

OFFICIAL PUBLICATIONS AND NEWSPAPERS

Boletín de la Biblioteca del Congreso de la Nación.

Constitución Política de la República Argentina. (1853).

Constitución Política de la República Argentina. (1949).
Constituciones Provinciales Argentinas.
Diarios de Sesiones de la Cámara de Diputados.
Diarios de Sesiones de la Cámara de Senadores.
Diarios de Sesiones de la Convención Constituyente de 1957.
Leyes Nacionales.
Parlamento Argentino.
Poder Legislativo de la Nación Argentina.
Clarín.
La Nación.
La Prensa.

INDEX

Agrarian reform, 36, 79, 80

aguinaldo decree, 61

Alem, Leandro, founder of the Republican Party, 5; founder of the Civic Union of Youth, 8; President of the UCJ Executive Committee, 10-11; founder of the UCR, 13-14; biographical sketch, 16-18; and revolt of 1893, 20; schoolmate of Roque Sáenz Peña, 25

Alende, Oscar, leader of a UCRI faction in 1963, 96-97; UCRI presidential nominee in 1963, 100-101; loser of the 1963 election, 103; and struggle for control of the UCRI, 104-105

Alianza Demócrata Socialista, 47-49

Alsina, Adolfo, 4-5, 14, 16-17

Alvear, Marcelo T., founder of the UCR, 13; UCR presidential nominee in 1922, 39; biographical sketch, 40; administration of 1922-1928, 40-44; reunification of the UCR, 46; UCR presidential nominee in 1932, 48; leader of the conservative faction of the UCR, 1930-1943, 51-57

Aramburu, Pedro, 71, 73, 80, 95, 103, 107

Assembly of Intransigent Radicalism, 62-63

Avellaneda, Nicolás, 4-5

azules, 27-28, 41

Balbín, Ricardo, expulsion from Congress, 67-68; UCR presidential nominee in 1951, 68-69; and the revolution of 1955, 71; founder of the UCRP, 74; UCRP presidential nominee in 1958, 80-83; and UCRP factionalism, 91; and the Guido administration, 97-98; and the selection of the UCRP presidential nominee in 1963, 101, 106

Begnis, Silvestre, 100-101

Castillo, Ramón, 57-58

Communist Party, member of the Democratic Union in 1945, 60; gain of several ex-UCR members, 70; votes for Frondizi in 1958, 82; and the Frondizi administration, 88-92

Concentración de Partidos de la Derecha, 44

Concilliation of Parties, 5, 17

Concordancia, 47-48

Congress of Latin American Neutral Nations, 38

Congress of Radical Youth, 55-56

corruption, 39, 44-45

Declaration of Avellaneda, 63, 72, 86, 90, 94, 115-116

Declaration of Chascomús, 90-91, 117-119

Democratic Union, 60-61

Ecclesiastic policy, 36

economic nationalism, of Irigoyen, 35-36, 43; of Alvear, 43; of Frondizi, 79, 85, 90; of Balbín, 80; of Illia, 107

educational policy, of Irigoyen, 34; of Balbín, 80; of Frondizi, 86

electoral abstention policy, 24, 27, 49-50, 62

Farrell, Edelmiro, 59-60

Federalists, 2-3

foreign policy, of Irigoyen, 37; of Alvear, 43; of Frondizi, 80, 92

Frigerio, Rogelio, 81-82, 88, 92, 101

Frondizi, Arturo, founder of the *Junta de Reafirmación Radical,* 62; leader of the MIR, 64; UCR vice-presidential nominee in 1951, 68-69; and the UCR convention of 1956, 71-72; and the 1957 split of the UCR, 73-75; biographical sketch, 77-78; pre-1958 program, 78-80; and the 1958 election, 81-83; administration of 1958-1962, 84-95; in exile, 97; support of Lima in 1963, 101; and UCRI split in 1963, 104-105

Fuerza de Orientación Radical de la Joven Argentina (FORJA), 51-52, 59-60

Garcia, Alfredo, 96

Gómez, Alejandro, 88

Gómez Machado, Hector, 104-105

Grupo de Oficiales Unidos (GOU), 59

Güemes, Adolfo, 48, 50

Guido, José María, administration of 1962-1963, 96-103

Illia, Arturo, 1963 program, 102; election of, 103; administration, 106-107

≞ OEMCO ≞